artfully
embroidered

Artfully Embroidered
Copyright © 2012 Naoko Shimoda
First published in the United States in 2014 by Interweave

interweave.com

A division of F+W, a content + eCommerce company
201 East Fourth Street
Loveland, CO 80537
interweave.com

The information in this book was originally published in the Japanese language by NHK
Publishing, Inc., Japan in the following title:
Shimoda Naoko no Shishu no Hon – Bag, Pouch, Komono

English language licensed by World Book Media, LLC, USA via Tuttle Mori Agency, Inc.,
Tokyo, Japan
English language translation & production by World Book Media, LLC, USA
Email: info@worldbookmedia.com

Translation: Namiji Hatsuse
English-language editor: Lindsay Fair
Design: Arati Devasher, www.aratidevasher.com
Cover embroidery motif based on original design by Heather Moore. All rights reserved.

Library of Congress
Cataloging-in-Publication Data not available at time of printing
ISBN-13: 978-1620337288

Printed in China
10 9 8 7 6 5 4 3 2 1

artfully embroidered

Motifs and Patterns for Bags and More

NAOKO SHIMODA

Author's Note

As a high school student in the 1970s, I was fascinated by fashion. I had no experience, but I studied fashion magazines every chance I could. I particularly loved foreign magazines, introducing exciting styles I had never dreamed of. There I discovered countless fashion treasures that set fire to my imagination. My eyes grew wide as they scanned magnificent silks and beads. The exotic flowers and animals that inspired these unfamiliar designs delighted my senses. I still remember how slowly I turned those precious pages, exhilarated by a fresh linen top with lily embroidery, a navy blouse with bright white embroidery, or a hand-embroidered wool bag. These were not the old boring techniques I'd learned in high school sewing class. From there, I went on to study advanced embroidery. But here's the secret they don't teach you in school: The key to embroidery is to put your heart into each stitch. When you work with loving care, that joy shows through in your designs. That's what makes embroidery fun and fulfilling.

NAOKO SHIMODA

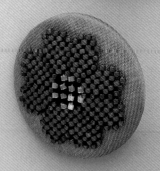

Contents

Denim Rose Bag

This bag is a study in contrasting texture and color. Layers of thin white fabric are folded and glued together to construct the stunning, three-dimensional roses. The dark indigo bag is also embellished with beautiful ribbon embroidery, then completed with handles of smooth white leather for maximum impact.

Instructions on page 54

Glitzy Granny Bag

Add a dose of glamor to your daily life with this sophisticated bag. Shiny silk taffeta is embellished with a combination of yarns, beads, and pearls to create a stunning bag that is spacious enough to hold all of your essentials.

Instructions on page 58

Scandinavian Tote

Great for fall and winter fashion, this rich-looking red linen tote features charcoal gray wool appliqué motifs that are embellished with traditional Scandinavian embroidery.

Instructions on page 63

Fair Isle Cross-Stitch Purse

With its charming round shape, this small handbag makes a lovely accessory for a special engagement. Here, clean modern design meets traditional embroidery. This white cotton bag is accentuated with red handles and matching red and black Fair Isle stitching.

Instructions on page 68

Japanese Garden Bag

This classic Japanese style satchel boasts a simple, inventive shape that delights the eye. A variety of cotton and linen threads, plus raffia, are used to craft the raised floral embroidery. Comfortable-to-carry, this collapsible shoulder bag conveys serene elegance.

Instructions on page 72

Floral motif based on design by Heather Moore.

1

2

Colorful Coin Purses

These adorable little pouches are well-designed: Each bag is
constructed with a fusible foam stabilizer foundation, allowing it
to stand up when the clasp is open. Variation 1 is decorated with
embroidery sampler motifs, variation 2 is worked with a variegated
embroidery floss, and variation 3 features a festive floral motif.
Choose your favorite variation, or design your own!

1. Scandinavian Sampler
2. Variegated Starbursts
3. Floral Folk Motif

Instructions on page 76

3

Goldfish Azuma Bag

A variety of materials make up the details of this winning design. Organdy appliqué goldfish, gracefully swimming through swaying raffia seaweed, exhale chain stitch cotton bubbles. You can't help but move self-assuredly with this creative carryall at your side.

Instructions on page 80

16

Sequined Knot Bag

This Azuma style bag is lightweight and distinctively fashionable. Appropriately placed square iridescent sequins make the polka dot pattern all the more dazzling.

Instructions on page 84

White Flower Straw Bag

This striking day bag refuses to go unnoticed. A three-dimensional flower stitched in soft white cotton adorns black straw. Easy-to-attach stylish handles make this the perfect summer tote when you want to look great on the go.

Instructions on page 87

Beaded Brooches

Express your innovative style with these beaded brooches. A soluble canvas sheet makes it easy to embroider on plainweave fabrics. Later, simply dissolve the canvas in warm water, leaving behind beautiful glass beads on linen.

Instructions on page 89

1

2

3

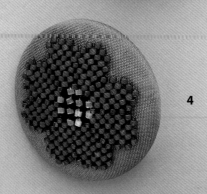

4

5

Appliqué Sampler Tote

This hand-woven, thick natural cotton is a traditional favorite among fashionistas. Time-honored Asian style becomes delightfully current when you introduce in-vogue appliqué. White handles and piping further enliven this fresh spring look.

Instructions on page 93

Raffia Rainbow Tote

This brightly colored
square tote redefines
chic. The colorful pattern
is embroidered in raffia,
a shred-resistant natural
material made
from palm leaves.

Instructions on page 98

Ribbon Flower Evening Bag

This small silk purse adds artistic flavor to your night on the town. Hand-stitched ribbon daisies finish the Bohemian look. Whether you're out in New York or Tokyo, this convenient accessory expresses attractive, versatile style.

Instructions on page 102

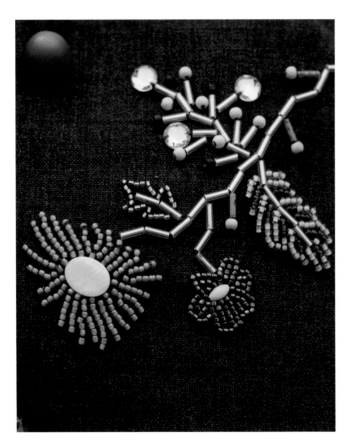 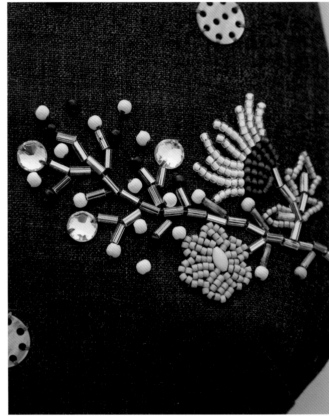

Beaded Wool Purse

Cast an air of exquisiteness with this awe-inspiring handbag. Glass beads and rhinestones shine in the light as you move. Dress an outfit up or down with this multifaceted look.

Instructions on page 105

Striped Clutch & Floral Wallet

Don't feel like carrying a big bag? Try these enchanting cases. Two inside pockets secure your bills and other essentials for a night on the town. The striped clutch on the left showcases a variety of embroidery techniques. The floral wallet on the right is embroidered with freshwater pearls and black onyx beads, revealing a brilliant picture when opened.

Instructions on pages 109 and 111

1

2

3

4

5

Classic Handkerchiefs

These vintage-style handkerchiefs make fine gifts. Use water soluble canvas to cross-stitch onto a handkerchief with ease. One small embroidered design is all you need for an arty yet sophisticated look.

Instructions on page 113

Skirt & Blouse Appliqué Motif

It's rewarding to transform old boring garments into fresh favorites. Iridescent sequins deliver a spectacular look. Create a new outfit simply by embroidering a matching stitch motif onto a blouse and skirt.

Instructions on page 116

Colorful Coin Purses...page 76

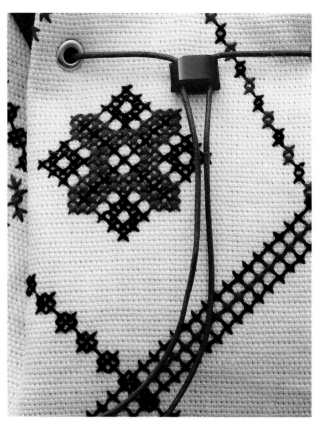

Fair Isle Cross-Stitch Purse...page 68

Colorful Coin Purses...page 76

Raffia Rainbow Tote...page 98

Colorful Coin Purses...page 76

Tools

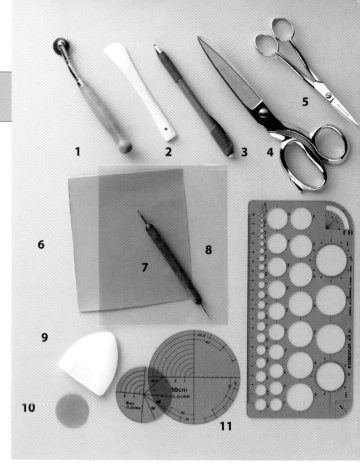

1. **Tracing wheel:** Use in conjunction with colored chalk paper to transfer marks from the pattern onto fabric.

2. **Hera marker:** Temporarily mark fabrics by creating a crease.

3. **Fabric safe mechanical pencil:** For tracing templates or marking fabric.

4. **Fabric shears:** Use a large, sharp pair of scissors for cutting fabric.

5. **Thread clips:** Use a small pair of scissors for cutting thread.

6. **Colored chalk paper:** Also known as dressmaker's tracing paper, this paper transfers colored chalk marks to the fabric when pressure is applied.

7. **Tracer pen:** Use the sharp tip to transfer small marks and thin lines to the fabric.

8. **Cellophane:** When using colored chalk paper to transfer marks to the fabric, use a thick sheet of cellophane to prevent damage to the paper template. Place the colored chalk paper on top of the fabric, arrange the paper template in position, then cover with cellophane before tracing.

9. **Chalk:** Use to draw seam allowances on fabric.

10. **Rubber:** Use a small piece of rubber to grab the embroidery needle and pull it out of the fabric if it gets stuck.

11. **Circle templates:** Different sizes of circle templates are useful for drawing appliqué and embroidery designs.

Other Tools You'll Need

Ruler/measuring tape: Use to measure out fabric and add seam allowances.
Quick-dry tacky glue: Use to construct projects with hardware, such as clasps and pins.
Embroidery needles: There are several different types of embroidery needles available, so choose one that corresponds with your style of stitching and weight of thread.

Hardware

Metal eyelets, grommets, and studs are a great way to add durability and a professional look to your bags.

Installing hardware may seem intimidating, but kits are available that make the process quick and easy. The kits will include everything you need, from the hardware itself to the hammer and metal plates used for installation.

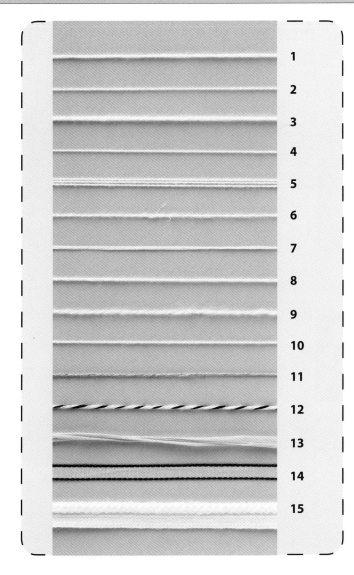

A wide variety of thread is used throughout this book, from traditional embroidery floss to more unconventional materials like raffia and kite string. This visual guide compares the different threads used in the book.

1 **Cotton Embroidery Floss #25 (DMC):** This is the most commonly used embroidery floss on the market today. It is made from long-staple mercerized cotton and composed of six strands that can be easily separated.

2 **Pearl Cotton #8 (DMC):** This 100% mercerized cotton thread has a lustrous appearance and feel.

3 **Retors Mat (DMC):** This thick and soft yarn-like thread is often used for tapestry embroidery. This thread is not mercerized, so it does not have a shiny appearance.

4 **Crochet Thread #30 (DMC Cebelia):** This three-ply crochet thread is made from combed cotton and is known for its brilliance and strength.

5 **Blomstergarn (DANSK):** Also known as Danish Flower Thread, this 100% cotton thread has a matte finish, making it popular for historical embroidery.

6 **Linen Embroidery Floss:** This 100% linen thread has a natural matte finish and is perfect for projects with a rustic look.

7 **Cotton Gima (Avril):** Translated from the Japanese, gima literally means "fake linen." This 100% cotton thread has a paper-like texture, but it grows softer each time it is washed.

8 **Hand Quilting Thread:** Use an extra-long staple cotton thread created specifically for hand quilting. Many hand quilting threads have a waxy finish to add strength and prevent tangles.

9 **Crewel Wool (Appleton):** This 100% wool yarn is used for crewel embroidery.

10 **Kite String:** Use ¼" (0.5-0.6 cm) wide cotton string.

11 **Linen Cord:** This cord possesses a natural texture and appearance. I used 16/3 weight linen cord for the projects within this book.

12 **Cotton Twist Yarn (Avril):** This 100% cotton yarn is twisted for a multicolored effect. Many different manufacturers offer cotton twist yarns. Just be sure to choose one that is suitable for embroidery, such as a fingering-weight yarn.

13 **Raffia (Ishii Craft):** See page 44 for details on this natural fiber similar to straw.

14 **Ribbon (La Droguerie):** Various types of ribbon can be used to create elegant, three-dimensional designs. Flat ribbon, such as the one pictured at left, works well for embroidery.

15 **Piping (MOKUBA):** Used as an edging for home decor accessories, fabric piping can also be used to trim bags.

Interfacing

The projects in this book do not require the use of an embroidery hoop or frame. Instead, interfacing is applied to the fabric to add strength and allow for easy embroidery. Different types of interfacing are used to provide structure and support to the projects included in this book. It is essential to use the correct interfacing to achieve professional-looking results. This guide explains how different types of interfacings are used to create various effects.

1. **Medium-weight fusible interfacing:** Composed of bonded man-made fibers, this type of interfacing can be ironed onto your fabric to provide a firm finish.

2. **Lightweight fusible interfacing:** Thinner than medium-weight fusible interfacing, this material provides support but maintains a fabric's soft feel.

3. **Featherweight fusible interfacing:** As the thinnest fusible interfacing available, this material is designed for sheer and lightweight fabrics. Rather than lining an entire piece of fabric as with other interfacings, I apply this material solely to the areas being embroidered.

4. **Medium-weight fusible interfacing + heavyweight fusible interfacing:** Look for a heavyweight fusible interfacing with the texture of firm felt. When I want to create a bag with a firm shape, I adhere medium-weight fusible interfacing to the fabric before embroidering. Then, I add a layer of heavyweight interfacing to add extra support.

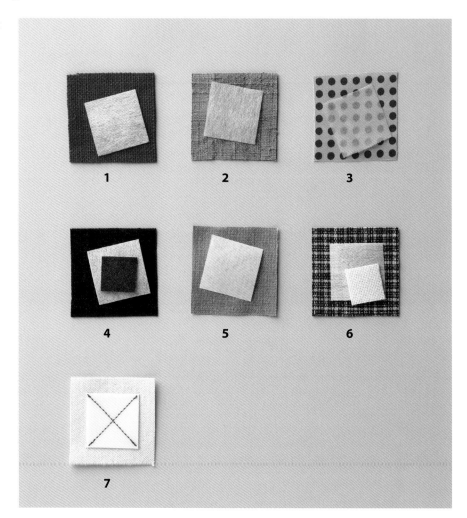

5. **Double-sided fusible interfacing:** Useful in appliqué, this interfacing has glue on both sides, allowing you to attach appliqué fabric to background fabric without the need for pins.

6. **Medium-weight fusible interfacing + fusible canvas:** Traditionally used in tailoring, canvas interfacing provides shape and structure. I often combine this material with medium-weight fusible interfacing to provide a project with extra support. Adhere the medium-weight fusible interfacing to the entire fabric, then add the fusible canvas interfacing to areas that receive a lot of wear and tear, such as bag openings.

7. **Fusible foam stabilizer:** Made from polyethylene foam, this material can be used to create bags with a rigid shape. I often use this material to line the bottom of my bags. To attach, adhere the foam stabilizer to the wrong side of the fabric, then stitch through both layers as shown.

WAYS TO USE INTERFACING

When you're using a thin fabric and want to maintain its soft look and feel, adhere featherweight fusible interfacing to the wrong side of the bag fabric behind the embroidered area only.

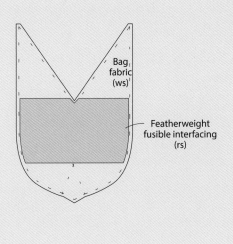

Bag fabric (ws)

Featherweight fusible interfacing (rs)

When you want to give the entire bag a firm shape, apply lightweight or medium-weight fusible interfacing to the wrong side of the fabric, then embroider. After the embroidery is complete, add a layer of heavyweight interfacing to each piece.

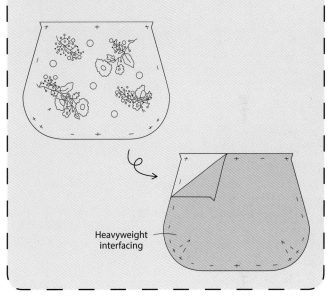

Heavyweight interfacing

When you want to reinforce the handle attachment area, apply a 2" (5 cm) wide strip of fusible canvas interfacing to the lining along the bag opening.

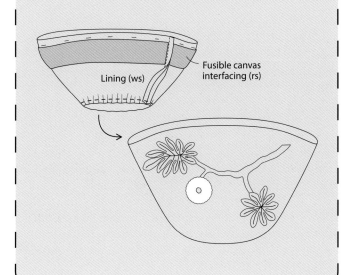

Lining (ws)

Fusible canvas interfacing (rs)

When you want to reinforce certain areas, such as the bottom or gusset, adhere fusible foam stabilizer to the desired area only. Stitch in the ditch on the right side to secure the fusible foam stabilizer in place.

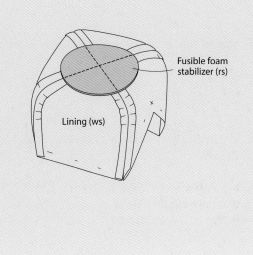

Fusible foam stabilizer (rs)

Lining (ws)

How to Appliqué

A few of the projects in this book use double-sided fusible interfacing, a material that makes the appliqué process quick and easy. Double-sided fusible interfacing has adhesive on one side and paper on the other. You'll use an iron to adhere the adhesive side of the interfacing to the wrong side of your appliqué fabric. Then, simply peel of the paper and stitch the appliqué piece in place on your foundation fabric. This special material allows you to appliqué easily without the need for tons of pins.

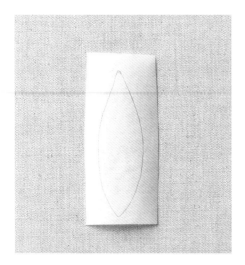

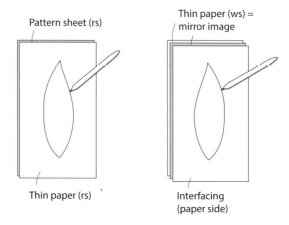

Pattern sheet (rs)

Thin paper (ws) = mirror image

Thin paper (rs)

Interfacing (paper side)

1   Trace the template onto a thin sheet of paper. Flip the template over so the mirror image is facing up. Trace the mirror image of the template onto the paper side of the interfacing. It may be helpful to use a lightbox for tracing. Note: It is very important to trace the mirror image in order for the design to appear correctly when complete. The interfacing will be attached to the wrong side of your fabric, so you'll need to draw the designs in reverse.

2 Trim the interfacing into shape, leaving about ¼" (0.5 cm) around all edges.

Interfacing (paper side)

3 Align the adhesive side of the interfacing with the wrong side of the appliqué fabric. Use an iron to adhere the interfacing to the fabric.

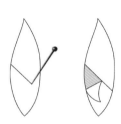

4 Trim the fabric into shape along the finishing lines. Use a pin to slash the paper side of the interfacing at the center of the appliqué. Peel off the paper, starting from the center and working outwards. This technique allows the paper to be removed easily and prevents damage to the fabric along the edges. Once the paper has been removed, you'll see that the wrong side of the appliqué fabric has been coated with adhesive.

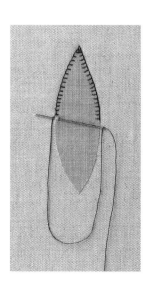

5 Align the adhesive side of the interfacing with the right side of the foundation fabric. Use an iron to activate the adhesive and adhere the interfacing to the fabric. Stitch around the appliqué piece as noted in the individual project instructions.

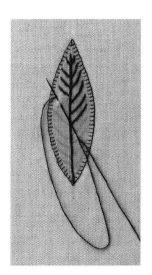

6 Transfer any remaining embroidery motifs to the appliqué piece using a fabric safe mechanical pencil. Embroider as noted in the individual project instructions.

How to Embroider with Raffia

Raffia is a natural fiber that is produced from the leaves of the raffia palm, a plant native to Madagascar. Artificial versions made from paper or synthetic materials are also available, but I recommend using genuine raffia for the best results. Authentic raffia maintains vivid color when dyed, possesses a soft texture, and resists shredding, even under pressure.

WIDTH

Raffia is available in a variety of widths. Experiment with different widths based on your individual design. The photo below shows three different widths of raffia.

a One wide piece of raffia: Use this width when you want a soft look, like with flowers.

b One thin piece of raffia: Use this width for more delicate embroidery.

c One split piece of raffia (strands separated from a): Use this width for heavily embroidered areas, such as satin stitch leaves.

HOW TO EMBROIDER FLOWERS WITH RAFFIA

This technique is used for the Raffia Rainbow Tote on page 26.

1 Adhere medium-weight fusible interfacing to the wrong side of the fabric. Transfer the embroidery motif to the right side of the fabric. Use an eyeleteer to puncture a hole at the center of the circle. The hole will prevent the raffia from breaking due to friction during the embroidery process.

2 Prepare a piece of raffia approximately the width of a on page 44. Make one backstitch on the wrong side of the fabric and leave a 1¼" (3 cm) long tail. Draw the needle out on the right side of the fabric along the left side of the embroidery motif.

3 Reinsert the needle through the hole at the center of the circle. Repeat the process to make another stitch from the top to the center of the circle. Make three more straight stitches to fill the first quadrant of the circle. Embroider the remaining three quadrants of the circle, working clockwise. Weave the raffia under a few stitches on the wrong side to secure the end.

HOW TO EMBROIDER LEAVES WITH RAFFIA

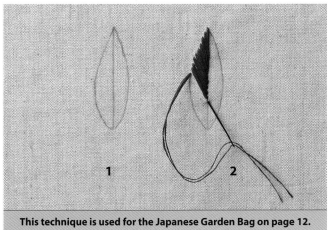

This technique is used for the Japanese Garden Bag on page 12.

1 Transfer the embroidery motif to the right side of the fabric.

2 Prepare a piece of raffia approximately the width of c on page 44. Make one backstitch on the wrong side of the fabric. Fill each half of the embroidery motif with satin stitch, working from top to bottom. Weave the raffia under a few stitches on the wrong side to secure the end.

HOW TO EMBROIDER PLANTS WITH RAFFIA

This technique is used for the Goldfish Azuma Bag on page 16.

1 Transfer the embroidery motif to the right side of the fabric. Work outline stitch using pearl cotton #8 to complete the stem. Prepare a piece of raffia approximately the width of b on page 44. Make one backstitch on the wrong side of the fabric. Embroider each section of the plant with straight stitch, working from the outside towards the center. Always insert the needle at the same point at the center. Weave the raffia under a few stitches on the wrong side to secure the end.

2 Completed view of embroidered plant.

How to Use Soluble Canvas

BEFORE YOU BEGIN

Water soluble canvas is similar to waste canvas, which is a product used in cross-stitch or beaded embroidery when it's difficult to count the fabric grain, like with plainweave fabrics. Water soluble canvas simply dissolves when submerged in warm water, unlike waste canvas, which needs to be removed thread by thread in a time consuming process. The projects in this book use DMC 14 count water soluble canvas, which is available in 8" x 8¾" (20 x 22 cm) sheets. Use a pointed embroidery needle with a sharp tip when stitching water soluble canvas.

FOR CROSS-STITCH MOTIFS

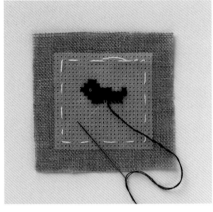

1 Cut a piece of canvas slightly larger than the area to be embroidered. Baste the canvas to the embroidery fabric.

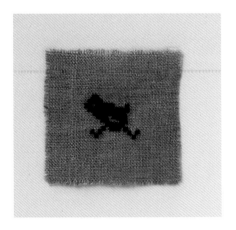

2 Embroider the motif using the holes in the canvas as a guide. For each row, work half cross-stitches, then return and cross each stitch, as shown on page 48.

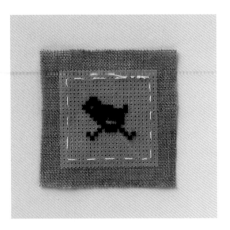

3 Once the embroidery is complete, remove the basting.

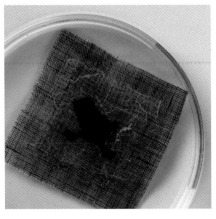

4 Submerge the embroidery in warm water for about 10 minutes, until the canvas dissolves.

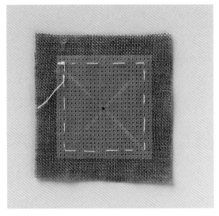

5 Let the embroidery air dry without squeezing excess water from the fabric. Iron from the wrong side to avoid flattening the embroidery.

FOR BEADED EMBROIDERY MOTIFS

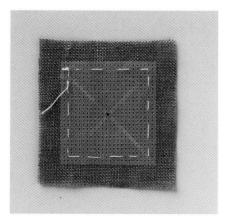

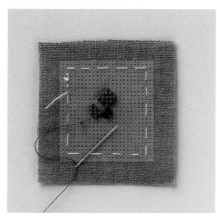

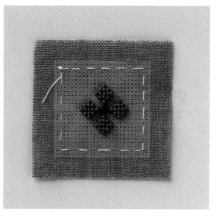

1 Cut a piece of canvas slightly larger than the area to be embroidered. Baste the canvas to the embroidery fabric.

2 Embroider the motif using the holes in the canvas as a guide. Add a bead onto the thread before completing each stitch, as shown on page 48.

3 Once the beaded embroidery is complete, remove the basting.

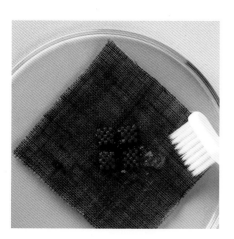

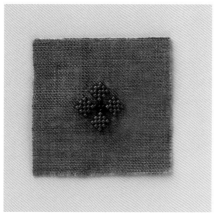

WATER SOLUBLE CANVAS

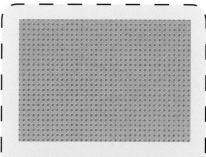

4 Submerge the embroidery in warm water for about 10 minutes, until the canvas dissolves. Use a toothbrush to remove excess canvas from the beads.

5 Let the embroidery air dry without squeezing excess water from the fabric. Iron from the wrong side to avoid cracking the beads.

Water soluble canvas is made from a chemical compound called polyvinyl alcohol (PVA). PVA is commonly used in cosmetic products; however, if you have a skin condition such as eczema, we recommend testing the canvas on a small area of skin before using.

HOW TO CROSS-STITCH WITH WATER SOLUBLE CANVAS

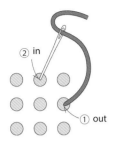 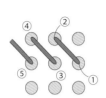 

1 Draw the needle out in the center of the hole, then reinsert the needle in the center of the next hole. This will ensure that all stitches are equal in size.

2 Work from right to left, making half cross-stitches.

3 Cross the stitches from left to right.

4 Working the two components of each stitch separately will produce neat and even results on the wrong side of the embroidery fabric.

HOW TO BEAD EMBROIDER WITH WATER SOLUBLE CANVAS

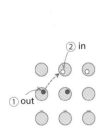 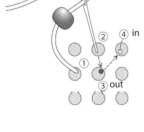 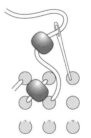 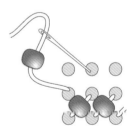

1 Draw the needle out at the edge of the hole.

2 String a bead onto the embroidery thread, then reinsert the needle at the edge of the next hole to complete a half cross-stitch.

3 After completing one row, turn the fabric upside down.

4 Work the next row in the same direction of the previous row. This technique will produce neat and even results on the wrong side of the embroidery fabric.

STRAIGHT STITCH

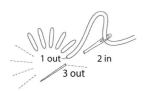

1 out   2 in
3 out

OUTLINE STITCH

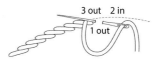

3 out   2 in
1 out

BACKSTITCH

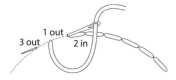

1 out
3 out   2 in

SATIN STITCH

LAZY DAISY STITCH

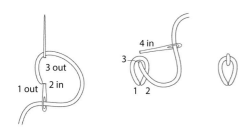

3 out
1 out   2 in
4 in
3
1   2

FRENCH KNOT STITCH (WRAP TWICE)

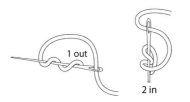

1 out
2 in

Wrap thread around needle # of times indicated (usually twice, unless otherwise noted).

Embroidery Tips

- You'll know you're using the right needle if it can be threaded easily and can pass through the fabric smoothly without causing the thread to tangle.

- Don't knot your thread when finished embroidering. Instead, leave a long thread tail, then secure by stitching over the thread tail on the wrong side of the work.

- Always iron embroidery on the wrong side of the work. It's alright to apply a bit of pressure when ironing, but I recommend covering the ironing board with a thick towel first to avoid flattening the embroidery.

FLY STITCH

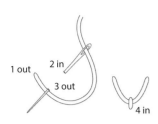

SINGLE FEATHER STITCH

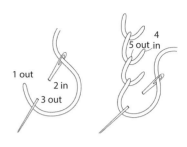

DOUBLE FEATHER STITCH

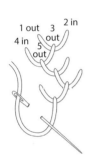

CHAIN STITCH

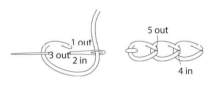

OPEN CHAIN STITCH

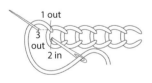

TURKEY STITCH

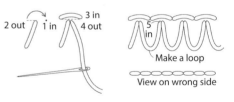

HERRINGBONE STITCH

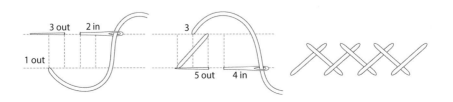

WIDE HERRINGBONE STITCH

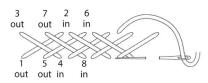

CLOSED HERRINGBONE STITCH

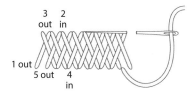

FISHBONE STITCH

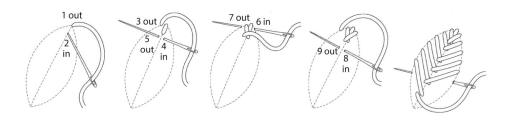

VANDYKE STITCH

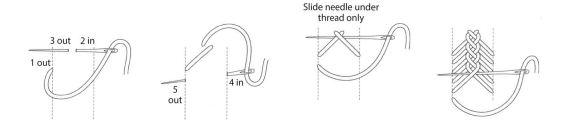

PORTUGUESE KNOTTED STEM STITCH

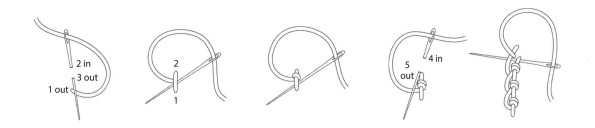

CABLE CHAIN STITCH

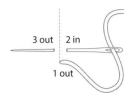 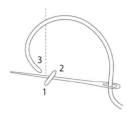 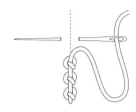 

3 out   2 in
1 out

3
1   2

Slide needle
under thread
only

CROSS-STITCH

Individual Stitches

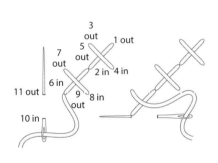

3
out   1 out
5
out
7
out
6 in   2 in   4 in
11 out   9
out   8 in
10 in

Horizontal Stitches

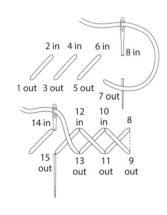 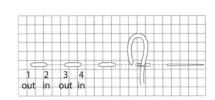

2 in   4 in   6 in   8 in
1 out   3 out   5 out
7 out

12   10
in   in   8
14 in
15   13   11   9
out   out   out   out

Vertical Stitches

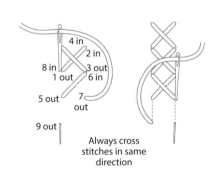 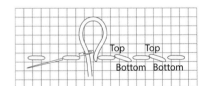

4 in
2 in
8 in   3 out
1 out   6 in
5 out   7
out
9 out

Always cross
stitches in same
direction

BLANKET STITCH

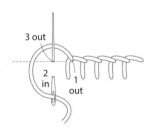

3 out
2
in   1
out

HOLBEIN STITCH

1   2   3   4
out   in   out   in

Top   Top
Bottom   Bottom

ATTACHING SEQUINS

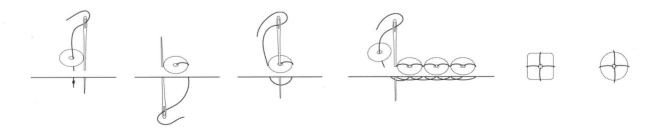

ATTACHING BEADS

Backstitch Method for Straight Line

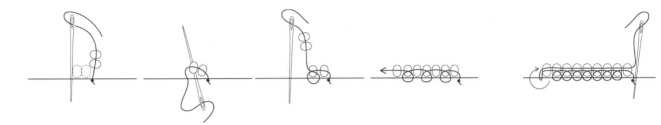

Couching Method to Fill an Area

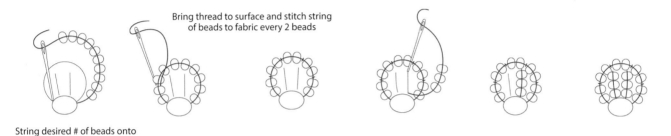

Bring thread to surface and stitch string of beads to fabric every 2 beads

String desired # of beads onto thread and insert through fabric

Couching Method for Circle

String desired # of beads onto thread, then insert through first 2 beads again

Stitch string of beads to fabric every 2 beads

RIBBON EMBROIDERY

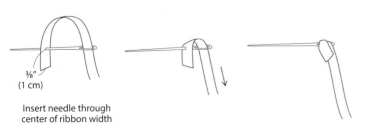

³⁄₈"
(1 cm)

Insert needle through center of ribbon width

RIBBON STITCH

Work from outside towards inside of motif

MATERIALS

Fabric
- Bag: 13¾" x 34" (35 x 86 cm) of indigo denim
- Lining: 13¾" x 34" (35 x 86 cm) of navy floral print cotton
- Roses: 13¾" x 35½" (35 x 90 cm) of white cotton lawn

Interfacing
- Medium-weight fusible: 13¾" x 34" (35 x 86 cm)
- Lightweight fusible: 13¾" x 34" (35 x 86 cm)
- Heavyweight fusible interfacing: 11¾" x 27½" (30 x 70 cm)
- Fusible foam stabilizer: 4¾" x 4¾" (12 x 12 cm)

Embroidery Supplies
- Linen cord in beige
- ¼" (0.5 cm) wide white taffeta ribbon in beige with black edges

Findings
- Twelve 1¼" (3 cm) diameter buttons or cover buttons (top half only)
- Two 27½" (70 cm) long pieces of ⅜" (0.8 cm) wide leather cord in white
- Four 3¼" (8.5 cm) long pieces of ⅜" (0.8 cm) wide leather cord in white
- Cotton stuffing

Tools
- Quick-dry tacky glue
- Eyeleteer

CUTTING INSTRUCTIONS

- **Seam allowance is not included. Add ⅝" (1.5 cm) seam allowance to all bag piece edges and ⅜" (1 cm) to all lining piece edges, unless otherwise noted.**
- Trace and cut out the side template on pattern sheet D. Cut out each piece according to the diagrams below.

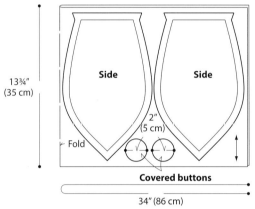

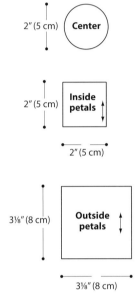

Cut 4 sides and 4 covered buttons without seam allowance from:
Bag fabric + medium-weight fusible interfacing

Cut 4 sides from:
Lining fabric + lightweight fusible interfacing

Cut 16 centers, 24 inside petals, and 24 outside petals all without seam allowance from:
Rose fabric

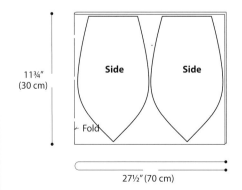

Cut 4 sides without seam allowance from:
Heavyweight fusible interfacing

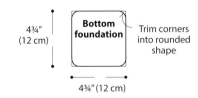

Cut 1 bottom foundation without seam allowance from:
Fusible foam stabilizer

CONSTRUCTION STEPS

Adhere the interfacing

Adhere medium-weight fusible interfacing to the wrong side of each bag side and lightweight fusible interfacing to the wrong side of each lining.

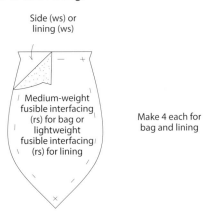

Side (ws) or lining (ws)

Medium-weight fusible interfacing (rs) for bag or lightweight fusible interfacing (rs) for lining

Make 4 each for bag and lining

Embroider the sides

Transfer the embroidery motif on pattern sheet D to each of the four sides. Embroider as indicated on the pattern sheet.

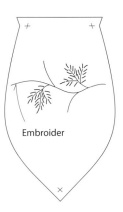

Embroider

Sew the bag together

1   With right sides together, sew two sides together starting at the edge and stopping at the seam allowance. Make clips into the curved seam allowance.

2   Repeat step 1 to attach the remaining two sides. Press seam allowances open.

3   Repeat steps 1–2 to sew the lining together, but use ½" (1.2 cm) seam allowance.

4   Turn the bag right side out. Adhere heavyweight fusible interfacing to the inside of the bag. Use your hands to ensure that the heavyweight fusible interfacing is securely adhered.

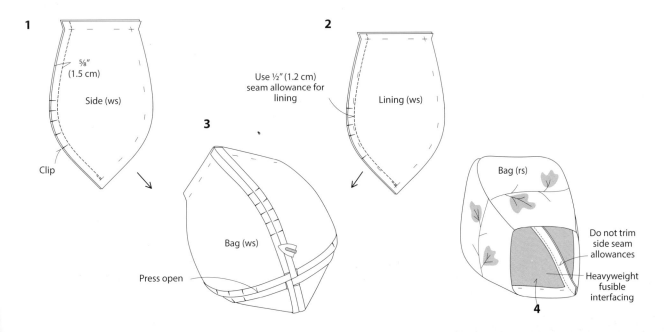

1

⅝" (1.5 cm)

Side (ws)

Clip

2

Use ½" (1.2 cm) seam allowance for lining

Lining (ws)

3

Bag (ws)

Press open

4

Bag (rs)

Do not trim side seam allowances

Heavyweight fusible interfacing

Attach fusible foam stabilizer

Adhere fusible foam stabilizer to the wrong side of the lining at the bottom, then stitch in the ditch on the right side of the lining to secure.

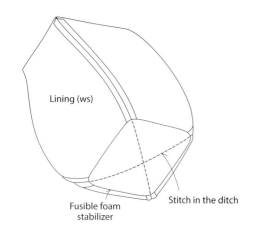

Lining (ws)

Fusible foam stabilizer

Stitch in the ditch

Make the loops and handles

1   For the loops, make four equally spaced holes at each end of each 3¼" (8.5 cm) long piece of leather cord using an eyeleteer.

2   For the handles, make two equally spaced holes at each end of each 27½" (70 cm) long piece of leather cord using an eyeleteer.

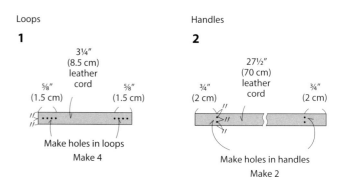

Loops
1

3¼" (8.5 cm) leather cord

⅝" (1.5 cm)   ⅝" (1.5 cm)

Make holes in loops
Make 4

Handles
2

27½" (70 cm) leather cord

¾" (2 cm)   ¾" (2 cm)

Make holes in handles
Make 2

Finish the bag

1   Sew the roses to the bag, as indicated on the pattern sheet. Make sure the stitching is not visible on the right side of the bag.

2   Insert the lining into the bag. Fold the seam allowances in and slip-stitch the bag and lining together around the opening. As you stitch, pull the lining down slightly so a bit of the bag fabric is visible on the inside.

3   Sew the loops to the bag using the linen cord.

4   Thread the handles through the loops. To make the covered buttons, running stitch and then pull the thread to gather the fabric around the button. Make four covered button halves. Align the handle so the covered button extends beyond the holes, then position another covered button on top. Slip-stitch the two halves of the covered button together. Repeat for the other handle.

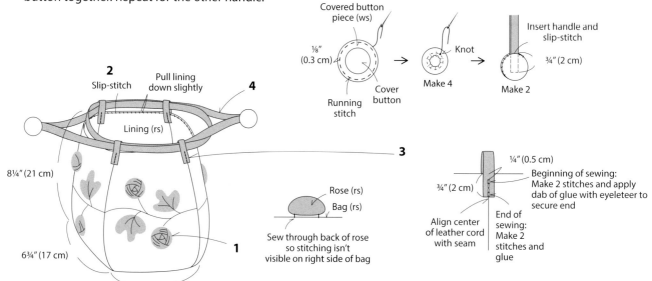

Covered button piece (ws)

⅛" (0.3 cm)

Running stitch

Cover button

Knot

Make 4

Insert handle and slip-stitch

¾" (2 cm)

Make 2

2
Slip-stitch

Pull lining down slightly

4

Lining (rs)

8¼" (21 cm)

6¾" (17 cm)

6¾" (17 cm)

1

3

Rose (rs)
Bag (rs)

Sew through back of rose so stitching isn't visible on right side of bag

¾" (2 cm)

Align center of leather cord with seam

¼" (0.5 cm)

Beginning of sewing: Make 2 stitches and apply dab of glue with eyeleteer to secure end

End of sewing: Make 2 stitches and glue

How to Make the Roses

1

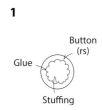

Glue a bit of stuffing to the center of each button.

2

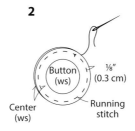

Layer two center pieces and running stitch using ⅛" (0.3 cm) seam allowance.

3

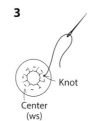

Pull the thread to gather the fabric around the button, then knot.

4

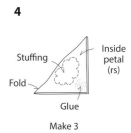

Make 3

Fold each inside petal in half to form a triangle. Insert stuffing between the two layers of fabric and glue the edges closed.

5

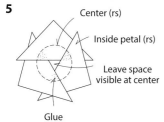

Glue three folded inside petals to each rose center.

6

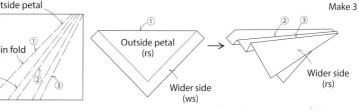

Make 3

Fold each outside petal as shown in the diagrams. Do not draw fold lines on the fabric.

7

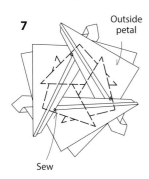

Hand sew three folded petals to each piece from step 5. Note: The stitching should not be visible on the finished rose.

8

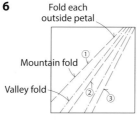

Trim excess fabric, leaving ⅝" (1.5 cm) seam allowances, around rose centers. Running stitch using ¼" (0.5 cm) seam allowance.

9

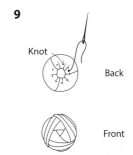

Pull the thread to gather the fabric around the button, then knot.

MATERIALS

Fabric
- Bag: 31½" x 35½" (80 x 90 cm) of beige silk taffeta
- Lining: 31½" x 35½" (80 x 90 cm) of black and white textured print
- Binding: 9¾" x 17" (25 x 43 cm) of black textured solid

Interfacing
- Lightweight fusible: 31½" x 35½" (80 x 90 cm)
- Medium-weight fusible: 31½" x 35½" (80 x 90 cm)

Embroidery Supplies
- Kite string in white
- Sashiko thread in gray
- Linen embroidery floss in gray and black
- Cotton twist yarn in black/natural combination
- Buttonhole thread in black

Beads
- Forty-seven 5 mm freshwater pearls in gray
- Seven 5 x 10 mm faceted marquise beads in black onyx
- Two hundred and fifty 11/0 glass seed beads in matte nickel (such as Miyuki Delica)

Handle Findings
- Two 10¼" (26 cm) long pieces of 1½" (4 cm) wide grosgrain ribbon in black
- Two 19¾" (1.8 cm) long pieces of ¹⁄₁₆" (0.2 cm) wide rope
- Four ¾" (1.8 cm) wide metal rectangular rings

CUTTING INSTRUCTIONS

- **Seam allowance is not included. Add ⅜" (1 cm) seam allowance to all piece edges, unless otherwise noted.**
- Trace and cut out the front/back and gusset templates on pattern sheet A. Cut out each piece according to the diagrams below.
- Note: For the front/back, cut out two 11¾" x 24¾" (30 x 63 cm) rectangles each of bag fabric and lightweight fusible interfacing. You will interface and embroider each piece before trimming into shape using the template.
- Cut out the following pieces, which do not have templates, according to the measurements below:
  – Bias strips: 1¾" x 10¼" (4.5 x 26 cm) of binding fabric

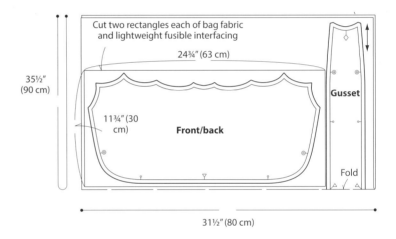

Cut two rectangles each of bag fabric and lightweight fusible interfacing

24¾" (63 cm)

35½" (90 cm)

11¾" (30 cm)

Front/back

Gusset

Fold

31½" (80 cm)

Cut 2 front/back and 1 gusset from each:
Bag fabric (cut as rectangles), lightweight fusible interfacing (cut as rectangles), lining fabric, medium-weight fusible interfacing

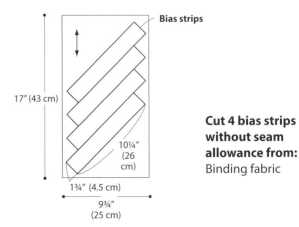

Bias strips

17" (43 cm)

10¼" (26 cm)

1¾" (4.5 cm)

9¾" (25 cm)

Cut 4 bias strips without seam allowance from:
Binding fabric

CONSTRUCTION STEPS

Adhere the interfacing

1 Adhere a rectangular lightweight fusible interfacing piece to the wrong side of both rectangular front/back pieces.

2 Adhere medium-weight fusible interfacing to the wrong side of both front/back lining pieces.

3 Adhere lightweight fusible interfacing to the wrong side of the gusset. Adhere medium-weight fusible interfacing the wrong side of the gusset lining.

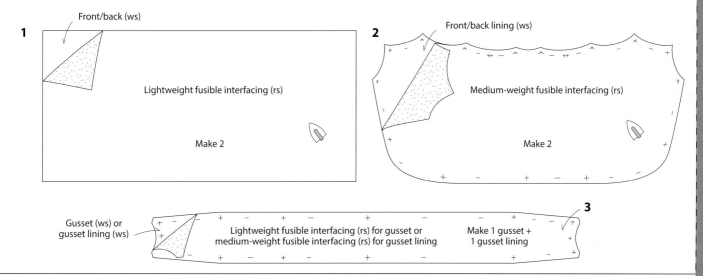

Embroider the front and back

1 Transfer the front embroidery motif on pattern sheet A to the front, then embroider and embellish with beads, as indicated on the pattern sheet on pattern sheet A. Refer to page 53 for instructions on attaching beads. Use the template to cut out the front, leaving ⅜" (1 cm) seam allowance.

2 Position the back embroidery motif on the back following measurements indicated in the diagram below and transfer. Follow same process as front to embroider, then trim the back.

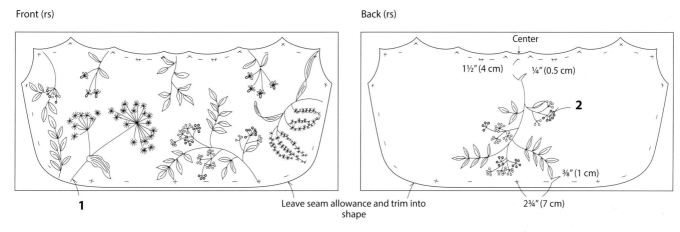

Attach the gusset

1   With right sides together, sew the gusset to both the front and back. Press the seam allowances towards the gusset.

2   Follow the same process to sew the lining together, but use a ½" (1.2 cm) seam allowance.

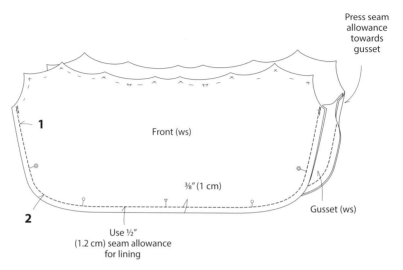

Press seam
allowance
towards
gusset

1

Front (ws)

⅜" (1 cm)

Gusset (ws)

2

Use ½"
(1.2 cm) seam allowance
for lining

Sew bag and lining together

1   Turn the bag right side out. Insert the lining into the bag.

2   With the bag and lining held together as one, fold the pleats as indicated on the pattern sheet and pin in place.

3   Sew around the front and back bag openings with ⅜" (1 cm) seam allowance to secure the pleats.

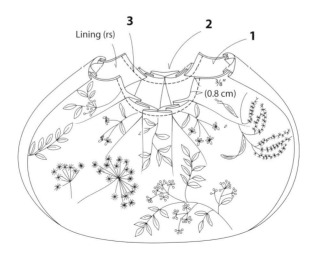

3

2

1

Lining (rs)

⅜"
(0.8 cm)

Bind the bag openings and gussets

1 Fold both long edges of the bias strips over ⅜" (1 cm) and press.

2 Open one of the folded edges and with right sides together, sew a bias strip to the front bag opening. Repeat process for back bag opening.

3 Wrap each bias strip around the seam allowance. Position each bias strip so it covers the stitching line (♡) on the lining. Stitch in the ditch to sew the binding to the lining. Trim excess binding.

4 Open one of the folded edges and with right sides together, align the center of a bias strip with one of the gussets (◇). Sew the bias strip to the gusset. Repeat process for the other gusset.

5 Repeat step 3 to sew the gusset binding to lining, but do not trim the excess binding.

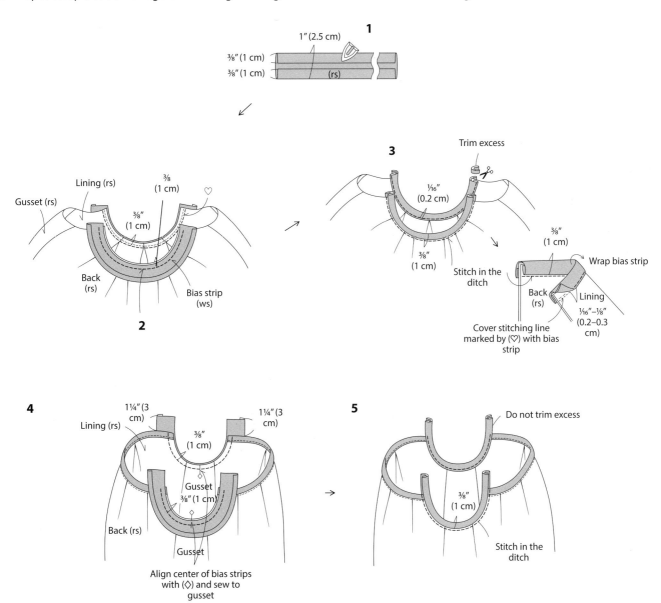

Attach metal rings to gusset bindings

1 Fold the short end of each gusset binding in ¼" (0.5 cm) and slip-stitch.

2 Thread a metal ring onto each gusset binding. Fold the binding and machine stitch 2–3 times to secure. Slip-stitch the sides and end of the folded binding using buttonhole thread.

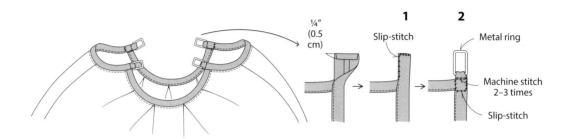

Make and attach the handles

1 Fold each 19¾" (50 cm) long piece of rope in half and make a mark 8" (20 cm) from the fold.

2 Fold each piece of grosgrain ribbon in half widthwise. Sew to create a tube, then turn right side out. Insert the folded rope into the grosgrain ribbon tube and sew in place 1¼" (3 cm) from the end of the ribbon. Trim the rope at the mark and insert inside the tube. Sew in place 1¼" (3 cm) from the end of the ribbon.

3 Thread each handle end through a metal ring and fold ⅝" (1.5 cm). Machine stitch 2–3 times to secure.

4 Slip-stitch the sides of the folded section.

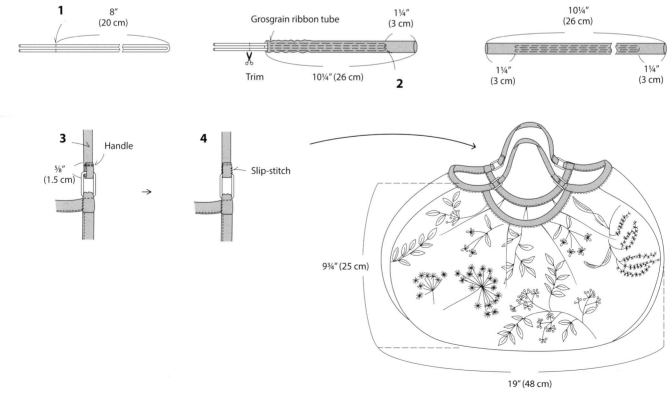

Scandinavian Tote SHOWN ON PAGE 10

MATERIALS

Fabric
- Bag: 17¾" x 35½" (45 x 90 cm) of red linen
- Lining: 26¾" x 33½" (68 x 85 cm) of black and beige polka dot polyester
- Appliqué: 10¾" x 11¾" (27 x 30 cm) of charcoal gray wool

Interfacing
- Medium-weight fusible: 17¾" x 35½" (45 x 90 cm)
- Lightweight fusible: 26¾" x 33½" (68 x 85 cm)
- Fusible canvas: 11¾" x 18¼" (30 x 46 cm)
- Fusible foam stabilizer: 5¼" x 9" (13 x 23 cm)

Embroidery Supplies
- DMC Retors Mat in black (2310) and ecru (ECRU)
- Linen cord in beige

Handle Findings
- Two 19" (48 cm) long pieces of ¾" (2 cm) wide ivory plastic chain handles

CUTTING INSTRUCTIONS

- **Seam allowance is not included. Add ⅜" (1 cm) seam allowance to all piece edges, unless otherwise noted.**
- Templates are not included for this project. Cut out each piece according to the diagrams below.

Cut 2 bags from each: Bag fabric and medium-weight fusible interfacing

Cut 4 handle attachments without seam allowance from: Medium-weight fusible interfacing

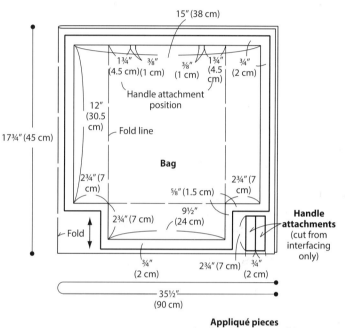

Cut 2 linings from each: Lining fabric and lightweight fusible interfacing

Cut 1 pocket from each: Lining fabric and lightweight fusible interfacing

Cut 1 of each appliqué piece without seam allowance from: Lightweight fusible interfacing

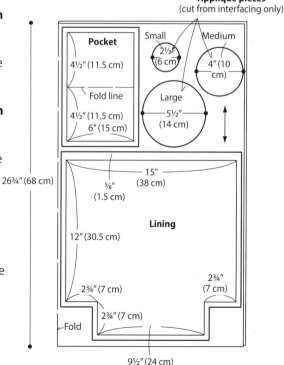

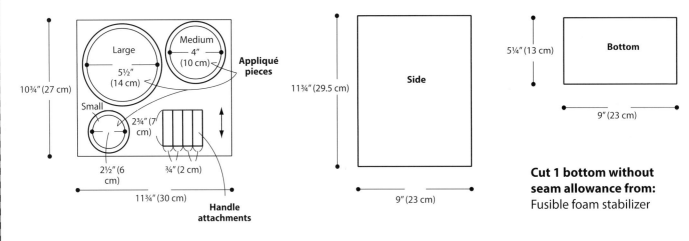

Large
5½"
(14 cm)

Medium
4"
(10 cm)

Appliqué
pieces

Small

2¾" (7 cm)

2½" (6 cm)

¾" (2 cm)

Handle
attachments

10¾" (27 cm)

11¾" (30 cm)

Side

11¾" (29.5 cm)

9" (23 cm)

Bottom

5¼" (13 cm)

9" (23 cm)

**Cut 1 bottom without
seam allowance from:**
Fusible foam stabilizer

Cut 1 of each appliqué piece from:
Appliqué fabric
**Cut 4 handle attachments without seam
allowance from:**
Appliqué fabric

**Cut 2 sides without seam
allowance from:**
Fusible canvas

CONSTRUCTION STEPS

**Sew using ⅜" (1 cm) seam allowance, unless
otherwise noted.**

Adhere the interfacing

1   Adhere medium-weight fusible interfacing to the wrong side of both bag pieces and lightweight fusible interfacing to the wrong side of both lining pieces.

2   Adhere lightweight fusible interfacing to the wrong side of the pocket.

3   Adhere medium-weight fusible interfacing the wrong side of all four handle attachments.

4   Adhere lightweight fusible interfacing to the wrong side of each appliqué piece.

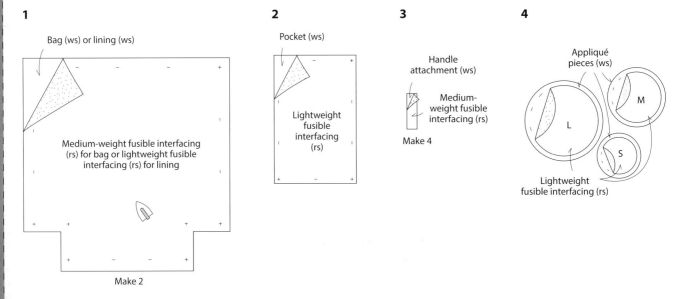

1

Bag (ws) or lining (ws)

Medium-weight fusible interfacing
(rs) for bag or lightweight fusible
interfacing (rs) for lining

Make 2

2

Pocket (ws)

Lightweight
fusible
interfacing
(rs)

3

Handle
attachment (ws)

Medium-
weight fusible
interfacing (rs)

Make 4

4

Appliqué
pieces (ws)

M

L

S

Lightweight
fusible interfacing (rs)

Appliqué and embroider

1 To turn the seam allowance under on each appliqué piece, running stitch using 1/16" (0.2 cm) seam allowance. Pull thread ends to gather into shape and press.

2 Appliqué each piece to the bag following placement shown in the diagram below. Transfer the embroidery motifs on pattern sheet B to the bag, then embroider as indicated on the pattern sheet. Refer to page 67 for lazy daisy fly stich with French knot instructions.

1

Running stitch
Interfacing
1/16" (0.2 cm)

2

¾" (2 cm)
2½" (6.5 cm)
1¼" (3 cm)
2½" (6.5 cm)
5¼" (13 cm)
3¼" (8.5 cm)

Sew the bag together

1 Align the two bag pieces with right sides together and sew along the bottom and sides using ¾" (2 cm) seam allowance.

2 Press the seam allowances open. For each gusset, align the bottom and side seam, then sew across perpendicularly to miter the corner.

3 Turn the bag right side out. Adhere each piece of fusible canvas interfacing to the inside of the bag.

1

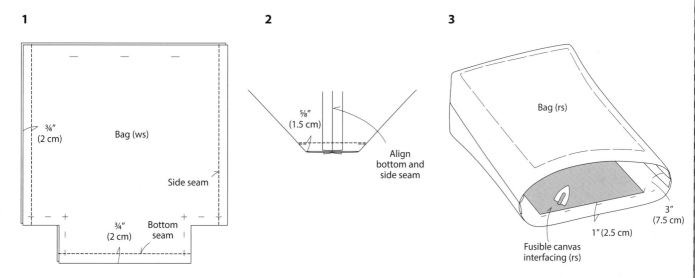

¾" (2 cm)
Bag (ws)
Side seam
¾" (2 cm)
Bottom seam

2

⅝" (1.5 cm)
Align bottom and side seam

3

Bag (rs)
3" (7.5 cm)
1" (2.5 cm)
Fusible canvas interfacing (rs)

Make the lining and pocket

1   Make the lining following the same process used to sew the bag together, but use ⅞" (2.2 cm) seam allowance.

2   Fold the pocket in half with right sides together and sew, leaving a 2½" (6 cm) opening. Turn right side out and fold the opening seam allowance in. Press.

3   Position the pocket on the back lining following placement shown in the diagram below. Topstitch using 1/32" (0.1 cm) seam allowance.

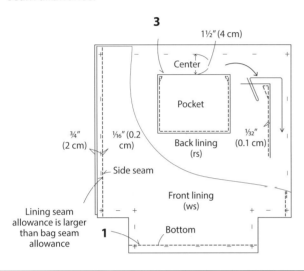

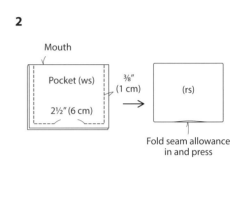

Attach the fusible foam stabilizer

1   Press the bottom and side seam allowances open and fold the bag opening seam allowance over ⅝" (1.5 cm) on both the lining and bag.

2   Adhere the fusible foam stabilizer to the wrong side of the lining at the bottom, then stitch in the ditch on the right side of the lining to secure.

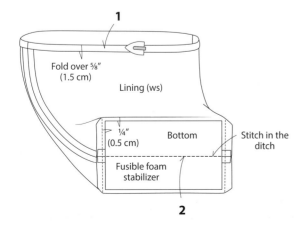

Make the handle attachments

1   Fold each long edge in ¼" (0.5 cm) and press. Topstitch using 1/32" (0.1 cm) seam allowance.

2   Thread each handle attachment through the end chain of a handle piece, fold, and sew across the short edge to secure.

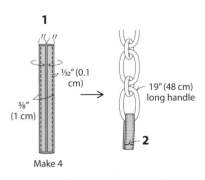

Finish the bag

1 Insert the lining into the bag. Fold the seam allowances in and slip-stitch the bag and lining together around the opening, leaving openings at the handle attachment positions. As you stitch, pull the lining down slightly so a bit of the bag fabric is visible on the inside.

2 Insert a handle attachment into each opening and topstitch 2–3 times to secure. Use red for your top thread and beige for your bottom thread.

3 Crease the bag along the fold lines, cover with a pressing cloth, and press.

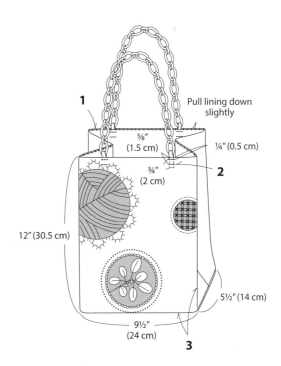

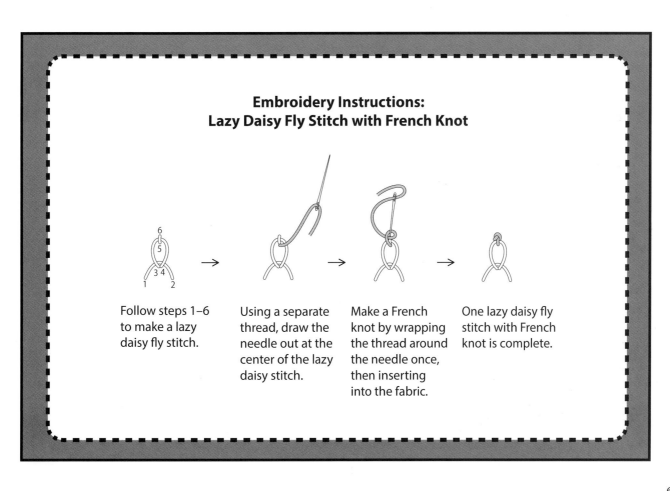

Embroidery Instructions:
Lazy Daisy Fly Stitch with French Knot

Follow steps 1–6 to make a lazy daisy fly stitch.

Using a separate thread, draw the needle out at the center of the lazy daisy stitch.

Make a French knot by wrapping the thread around the needle once, then inserting into the fabric.

One lazy daisy fly stitch with French knot is complete.

Fair Isle Cross-Stitch Purse SHOWN ON PAGE 11

MATERIALS

Fabric
- Bag: 8¼" x 22¾" (21 x 58 cm) of unbleached cotton/linen blend 22 count cross-stitch canvas
- Lining: 8¼" x 22¾" (21 x 58 cm) of orange silk taffeta

Interfacing
- Medium-weight fusible: 8¼" x 22¾" (21 x 58 cm)
- Lightweight fusible: 8¼" x 22¾" (21 x 58 cm)

Embroidery Supplies
- DMC cotton embroidery floss #25 in black (310) and brick red (3777)

Handle Findings
- Two 11¾" (29.5 cm) long pieces of ⅜" (1 cm) wide red leather cord
- 19¾" (50 cm) of ¹⁄₃₂" (0.1 cm) diameter red waxed cord
- One ¼" x ½" (0.7 x 1.2 cm) red cord lock
- Eight sets of ¼" (0.7 cm) diameter nickel eyelets

CUTTING INSTRUCTIONS

- **Seam allowance is not included. Add ⅜" (1 cm) seam allowance to all piece edges, unless otherwise noted.**
- Trace and cut out the bag template on pattern sheet B.
- Cut out each piece according to the diagrams below.
- Note: Cut out two rectangles each of bag fabric and medium-weight fusible interfacing. You will interface and embroider each piece before trimming into shape using the template.

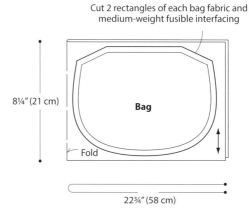

Cut 2 rectangles of each bag fabric and medium-weight fusible interfacing

8¼" (21 cm)

Bag

Fold

22¾" (58 cm)

Cut 2 bags from each:
Bag fabric (cut as rectangles), medium-weight fusible interfacing (cut as rectangles), lining fabric, and lightweight fusible interfacing

CONSTRUCTION STEPS

Sew using ⅜" (1 cm) seam allowance, unless otherwise noted.

Adhere the interfacing

1   Adhere a rectangular medium-weight fusible interfacing piece to the wrong side of both rectangular bag pieces.

2   Adhere lightweight fusible interfacing to the wrong side of each lining piece.

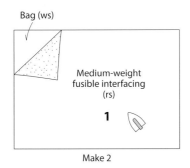

Bag (ws)

Medium-weight fusible interfacing (rs)

1

Make 2

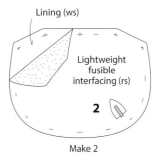

Lining (ws)

Lightweight fusible interfacing (rs)

2

Make 2

Embroider the bag

Use the cross-stitch charts on page 71 to embroider both the bag front and back. Once the embroidery is complete, use the bag template to trim the pieces into shape, leaving ⅜" (1 cm) seam allowance.

Leave seam allowance and trim into shape

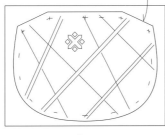

Front

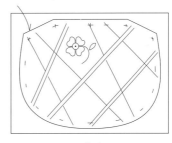

Back

Sew the bag together

1 Align the front and back with right sides together and sew, starting and stopping at the seam allowances, as indicated by the (☆).

2 Fold the bag opening seam allowance over ⅜" (1 cm) and press.

3 Press the seam allowance open.

4 Align the front and back lining with right sides together and sew, starting and stopping at the seam allowances, as indicated by the (☆). Use ½" (1.2 cm) seam allowance.

5 Fold the lining opening seam allowance over ½" (1.2 cm) and press.

6 Press the seam allowance open.

7 Turn the bag right side out. Insert the lining into the bag. Slip-stitch the bag and lining together around the opening. As you stitch, pull the lining down slightly so a bit of the bag fabric is visible on the inside.

8 Install the four outer eyelets, as indicated on pattern sheet B.

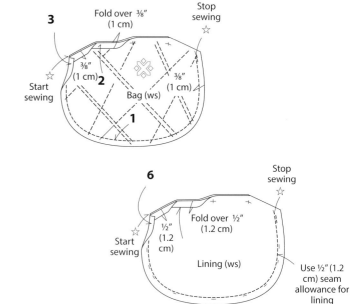

3 Fold over ⅜" (1 cm) · Stop sewing ☆ · ⅜" (1 cm) · Start sewing ☆ · ⅜" (1 cm) 2 · ⅜" (1 cm) · Bag (ws) · 1

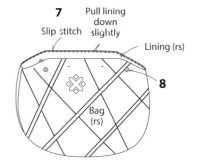

6 · Stop sewing ☆ · Fold over ½" (1.2 cm) · ½" (1.2 cm) · Start sewing ☆ · Lining (ws) · Use ½" (1.2 cm) seam allowance for lining

7 Pull lining down slightly · Slip stitch · Lining (rs) · Bag (rs) · 8

Make the pleats

1 Fold the pleats, as indicated on pattern sheet B and press.

2 Install the four inner eyelets, following placement indicated on pattern sheet B.

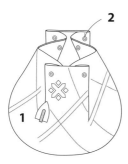

2 · 1

Finish the bag

1 Use the eyeleteer to make a hole ⅜" (1 cm) from each handle end. Thread the waxed cord through the eyelets and handles.

2 Thread the waxed cord ends through the cord lock. Make a knot at each cord end.

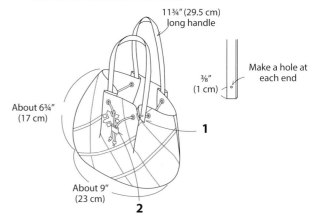

11¾" (29.5 cm) long handle · Make a hole at each end · ⅜" (1 cm) · About 6¾" (17 cm) · 1 · About 9" (23 cm) · 2

CROSS-STITCH CHARTS

Front

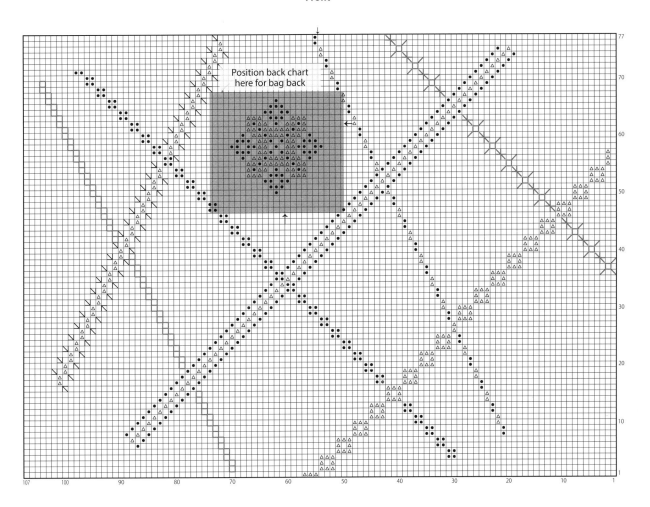

Position back chart here for bag back

Back

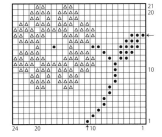

Use front chart pictured above, but replace the star motif with this flower motif.

Stitching Guide

Cross-Stitch

● = 310

△ = 3777

Holbein Stitch

◹ = 310

◥ = 3777

Fabric Count

1 stitch =

⊠ = 2 counts

2 counts

* Use 3 strands for all stitching.

MATERIALS

Fabric

- Bag: 14½" x 32¼" (37 x 82 cm) of unbleached linen
- Lining: 14½" x 32¼" (37 x 82 cm) of orange silk taffeta

Interfacing

- Featherweight fusible: 14½" x 32¼" (37 x 82 cm)
- Medium-weight fusible: 14½" x 32¼" (37 x 82 cm)

Embroidery Supplies

- A: DMC cotton embroidery floss #25 in black (310)
- B: DMC Retors Mat in black (2310)
- C: DMC Cebelia #20 in black (310)
- D: Linen embroidery floss in black
- E: DANSK Blomstergarn in black (16)
- F: Raffia in black

CUTTING INSTRUCTIONS

- **Seam allowance is not included. Add ⅜" (1 cm) seam allowance to all piece edges, unless otherwise noted.**
- Templates are not included for this project. Cut out each piece according to the diagram below.

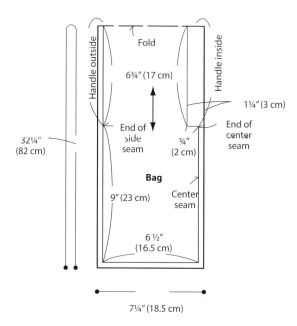

Cut 2 bags from each:
Bag fabric, medium-weight fusible interfacing, lining fabric, and featherweight fusible interfacing

CONSTRUCTION STEPS

Sew using ⅜" (1 cm) seam allowance, unless otherwise noted.

Adhere the interfacing

Adhere medium-weight fusible interfacing to the wrong side of both bag pieces and featherweight fusible interfacing to the wrong side of both lining pieces.

Medium-weight fusible interfacing or featherweight fusible interfacing

Make 2 each of bag and lining

Bag or lining (ws)

Sew the left and right halves together

Align the two bag pieces with right sides together and sew, starting and stopping at the end of the center seam, as indicated by the (☆). Repeat to sew the two lining pieces together.

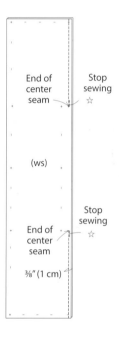

End of center seam

Stop sewing ☆

(ws)

Stop sewing ☆

End of center seam

⅜" (1 cm)

Embroider the bag

1   Press the seam allowances open on both the bag and lining.

2   Transfer the embroidery motif on pattern sheet B to the bag. Embroider as indicated on pattern sheet B.

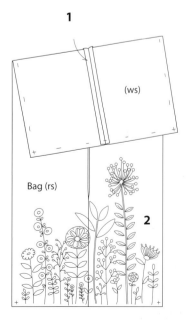

1

(ws)

Bag (rs)

2

Sew bag and lining together along handle insides

1 Align the bag and lining with right sides together. Start at one end of center seam (☆) and sew in a U-shape on the left half of the bag until you reach the other end of center seam (☆). Be careful not to catch the right half of the bag while you sew.

2 Trim the seam allowance to ⅜" (1 cm).

3 Make diagonal clips into the seam allowance at the corners.

4 Repeat steps 1–3 to complete the right half of the bag.

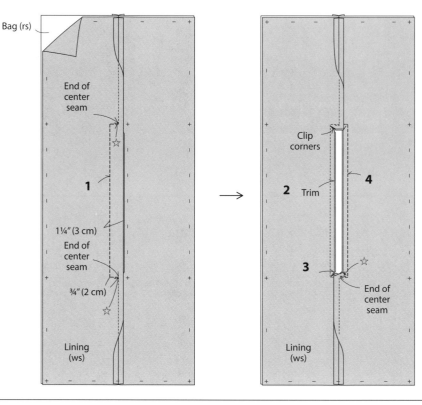

Sew bag and lining together along handle outsides

1 Turn the lining right side out through the handle.

2 Align the right half of the lining and bag with right sides together. Fold the left halves of the bag and lining out of the way so you do not catch them while sewing.

3 Sew together, starting and stopping at the end of the side seams (☆).

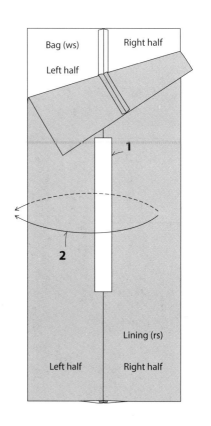

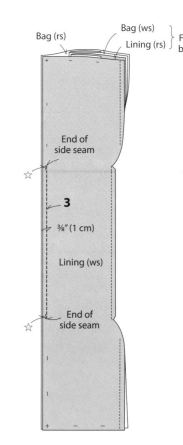

Sew bag and lining together along handle outsides (continued)

4 Turn right side out.

5 Repeat steps 2–4 to complete the left half of the bag.

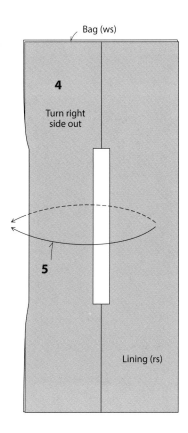

Bag (ws)

4

Turn right side out

5

Lining (rs)

Sew the lining together

Fold the bag in half to align the raw edges of the lining with right sides together. Pull the bag fabric out of the way so you don't catch it while sewing. Sew along the sides and bottom, leaving a 6″ (15 cm) opening to turn right side out.

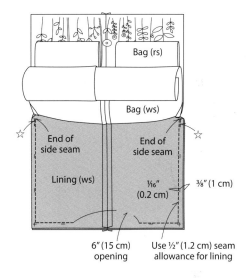

Bag (rs)

Bag (ws)

End of side seam

End of side seam

Lining (ws)

¹⁄₁₆″ (0.2 cm)

³⁄₈″ (1 cm)

6″ (15 cm) opening

Use ½″ (1.2 cm) seam allowance for lining

Finish the bag

1 Align the raw edges of the bag with right sides together and sew along the sides and bottom.

2 Turn the bag right side out and slip-stitch the opening closed.

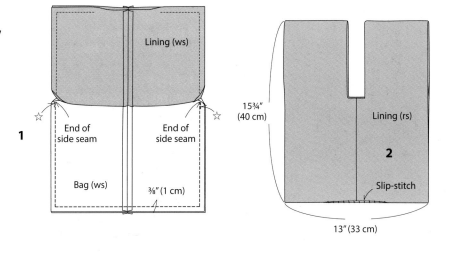

Lining (ws)

1

End of side seam

End of side seam

Bag (ws)

³⁄₈″ (1 cm)

15¾″ (40 cm)

Lining (rs)

2

Slip-stitch

13″ (33 cm)

MATERIALS (FOR ONE BAG)

Fabric

- Bag: 8" x 12¼" (20 x 31 cm) of tsumugi pongee or linen/silk blend in black, beige, or orange
- Lining: 8" x 12¼" (20 x 31 cm) of silk taffeta

Interfacing

- Medium-weight fusible: 12¼" x 15¾" (31 x 40 cm)
- Fusible foam stabilizer: 3⅛" x 3⅛" (8 x 8 cm)

Embroidery Supplies

- For Scandinavian Sampler:
  - Cotton gima in white
- For Variegated Starbursts:
  - DMC #8 pearl cotton in variegated terracotta (69)
- For Floral Folk Motifs:
  - DMC Cebelia #30 in A: yellow green (989)
  - DANSK Blomstergarn in B: red (302), C: bordeaux (315), D: yellow green (820), and E: light beige (904)
  - Appleton crewel wool in F: dark green (159), G: yellow green (425), H: peacock blue (485), I: blue (565), J: orange (626), K: mustard (844), L: dark purple (935), and M: rose pink (947)
  - Cotton gima in N: charcoal gray

Findings

- Coin purse frame: 2½" x 4¾" (6 x 12 cm) square silver frame with red, pearlescent beige, or ivory clasp

Tools

- Eyeleteer
- Pliers
- Glue
- Toothpick
- Fabric safe mechanical pencil

CUTTING INSTRUCTIONS

- **Seam allowance is not included. Add ⅜" (1 cm) seam allowance to all piece edges, unless otherwise noted.**
- Trace and cut out the front/back and side templates on pattern sheet C. Cut out each piece according to the diagrams below.
- Note: For the front/back, cut out two 6¼" x 8" (15.5 x 20 cm) rectangles each of bag fabric and medium-weight fusible interfacing. You will interface and embroider each piece before trimming into shape using the template.
- Cut out the following pieces, which do not have templates, according to the measurements below:
  - Bottom foundation: 3 ⅛" (8 cm) diameter circle of fusible foam stabilizer

Cut two rectangles each of bag fabric and medium-weight fusible interfacing

Center

Bag fabric + lining fabric: 8" (20 cm)

Front/back

Side

Fold

Medium-weight fusible interfacing: 15¾" (40 cm)

12¼" (31 cm)

Cut 2 rectangular front/backs from each:
Bag fabric and medium-weight fusible interfacing

Cut 2 front/backs from each:
Lining fabric and medium-weight fusible interfacing

Cut 2 sides from each:
Bag fabric and lining fabric

Cut 4 sides from:
Medium-weight fusible interfacing

Cut 1 bottom foundation without seam allowance from:
Fusible foam stabilizer

3⅛" (8 cm)

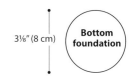

Bottom foundation

CONSTRUCTION STEPS

Sew using ⅜" (1 cm) seam allowance, unless otherwise noted.

Adhere the interfacing

1 Adhere a rectangular medium-weight fusible interfacing piece to the wrong side of each rectangular front/back pieces.

2 Adhere medium-weight fusible interfacing to the wrong side of each side, side lining, and front/back lining.

1   Make 2   Make 2   **2**   Make 2

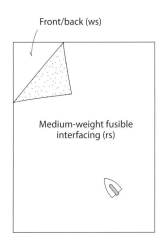

Front/back (ws)

Medium-weight fusible interfacing (rs)

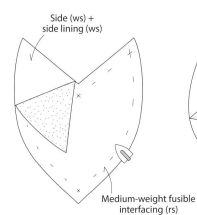

Side (ws) + side lining (ws)

Medium-weight fusible interfacing (rs)

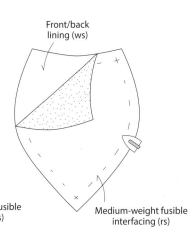

Front/back lining (ws)

Medium-weight fusible interfacing (rs)

Embroider the front/back

1 Transfer the embroidery motif on pattern sheet C to the front and back. (Note: Variations 1 + 2 use the same motif on both front and back, while variation 3 uses two different motifs.) Embroider as indicated on the pattern sheet. Do not embroider ¼" (0.5 cm) below the bag opening seam allowance.

2 Once the embroidery is complete, use the front/back template to cut out the front and back, leaving ⅜" (1 cm) seam allowance.

Do not embroider ¼" (0.5 cm) below the bag opening seam allowance

¼" (0.5 cm)

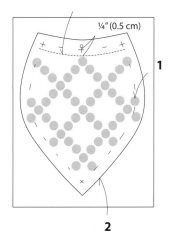

1

2

Sew the bag together

1 With right sides together, sew the front and one side together, starting and stopping at the seam allowances and making sure to backstitch (★). Cut notches into the curved seam allowance and press open.

2 Repeat step 1 to attach the back and remaining side. Follow the same process to sew the lining together.

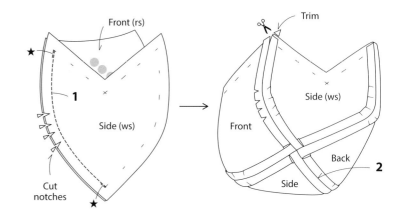

Attach bottom foundation

Adhere the bottom foundation to the wrong side of the lining, then stitch in the ditch on the right side of the lining to secure.

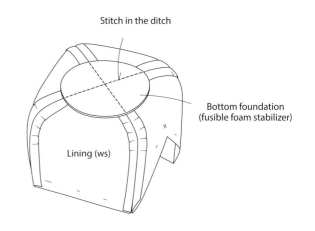

Attach the lining

1 With right sides together, insert the lining into the bag. Sew together, leaving a 2¾" (7 cm) opening. Clip the seam allowance at each side.

2 Turn right side out and slip-stitch the opening closed.

3 Mark the finishing line ¼" (0.5 cm) below the bag opening using a fabric safe mechanical pencil.

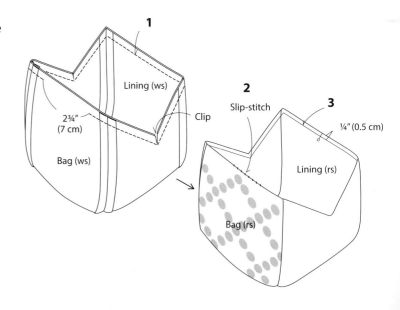

Install the coin purse frame

1. Trim the paper string so it is the width of the coin purse frame. Mark the center of the string.

2. Apply glue inside the grooves of the coin purse frame. Use a toothpick to evenly distribute the glue.

3. Insert the fabric into the grooves of the coin purse frame using an eyeleteer. For each side of the bag, start at the center and work your way outwards, making sure the center of the fabric is aligned with the center of the coin purse frame.

4. Follow the process used in step 3 to insert the paper string into the grooves of the coin purse frame on one side.

5. Use a pair of pliers to squeeze the fabric into the coin purse frame. Make sure to position a scrap of fabric between the coin purse frame and the pliers to protect the metal.

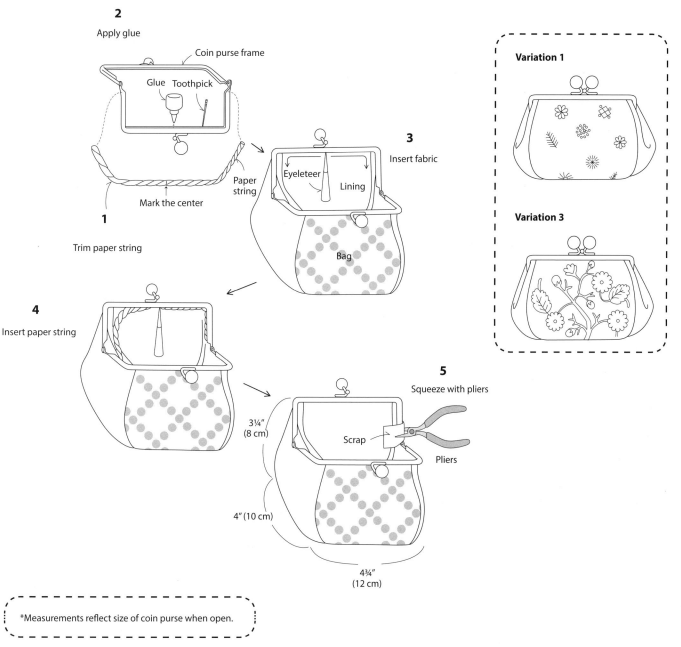

2 Apply glue

Coin purse frame

Glue   Toothpick

Paper string

Mark the center

1 Trim paper string

3 Insert fabric

Eyeleteer   Lining

Bag

Variation 1

Variation 3

4 Insert paper string

3¼" (8 cm)

4" (10 cm)

4¾" (12 cm)

5 Squeeze with pliers

Scrap

Pliers

*Measurements reflect size of coin purse when open.

Goldfish Azuma Bag SHOWN ON PAGE 16

MATERIALS

Fabric
- Bag: 23¾" x 40¼" (63 x 102 cm) of beige silk taffeta
- Lining: 23¾" x 40¼" (63 x 102 cm) of black and white cotton gingham
- Appliqué: 4¾" x 8" (12 x 20 cm) of black organdy

Interfacing
- Double-sided fusible: 4¾" x 8" (12 x 20 cm)

Embroidery Supplies
- Cosmo cotton embroidery floss #25 in A: dark gray (155), B: black (600), C: ivory (365), and D: gray (154)
- E: DMC pearl cotton #8 in dark beige gray (642)
- F: Raffia in green

Handle Findings
- Two 2" (5 cm) diameter bamboo rings

CUTTING INSTRUCTIONS

- **Seam allowance is not included. Add ⅜" (1 cm) seam allowance to all piece edges, unless otherwise noted.**
- Templates are not included for this project. Cut out each piece according to the diagram below.

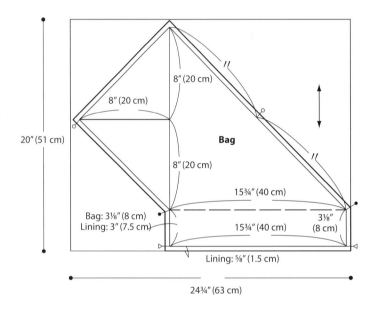

Cut 2 bags from each:
Bag fabric and lining fabric

CONSTRUCTION STEPS

Sew using ⅜" (1 cm) seam allowance, unless otherwise noted.

Sew the bag pieces together

Align the two bag pieces with right sides together and sew the diagonal and side seams. Make a clip into the corner seam allowance of the top bag piece only.

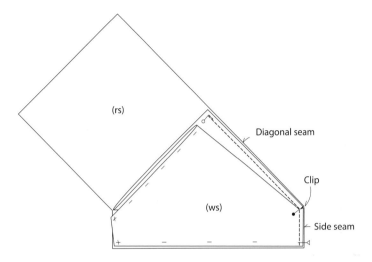

Appliqué and embroider the bag

1   Adhere double-sided fusible interfacing to the wrong side of the appliqué fabric. Transfer the mirror image of each goldfish appliqué to the interfacing, then cut along the outline. Adhere each goldfish appliqué to the bag following placement indicated on pattern sheet D. Appliqué and embroider as shown on the next page (also refer to pages 42–43 for appliqué instructions).

2   Embroider the plants and bubbles as indicated on pattern sheet D. Refer to pages 44–45 for instructions on embroidering with raffia.

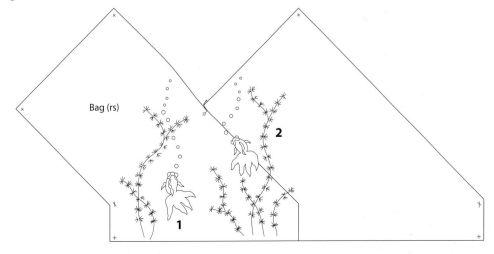

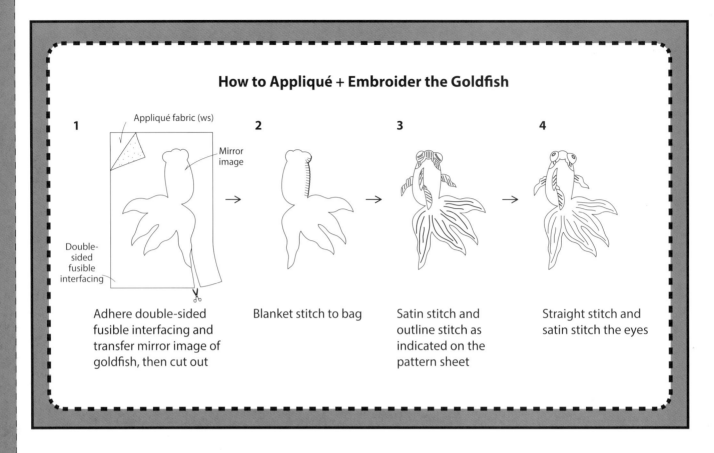

How to Appliqué + Embroider the Goldfish

1 Appliqué fabric (ws)

Mirror image

Double-sided fusible interfacing

Adhere double-sided fusible interfacing and transfer mirror image of goldfish, then cut out

2 Blanket stitch to bag

3 Satin stitch and outline stitch as indicated on the pattern sheet

4 Straight stitch and satin stitch the eyes

Sew the bag together

1 Follow the same process used on page 81 to sew the remaining diagonal and side seams. Press seam allowance open.

2 Sew across the bottom.

3 Sew the two lining pieces together along the diagonal and side seams. Sew across the bottom using ⅝" (1.5 cm) seam allowance and leave a 4" (10 cm) opening for turning right side out.

4 For each gusset, align the bottom and side seam, then sew perpendicularly to miter the corner. Repeat the process for the lining.

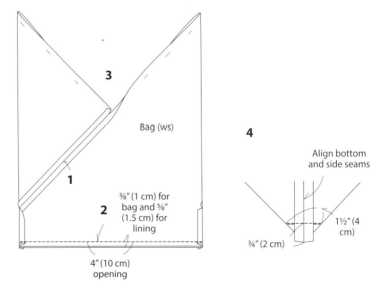

Bag (ws)

3

1

2 ⅜" (1 cm) for bag and ⅝" (1.5 cm) for lining

4" (10 cm) opening

4 Align bottom and side seams

1½" (4 cm)

¾" (2 cm)

Attach the lining

1   Align the bag and lining with right sides together and sew along the bag opening. Make sure to sew the right and left halves separately without stitching through the seam allowance.

2   Turn the bag right side out. Topstitch around the bag opening, pulling the lining down slightly as you stitch so a bit of the bag fabric is visible on the inside.

3   Slip-stitch the bottom opening closed.

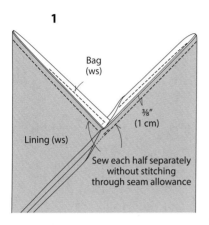

1

Bag (ws)

Lining (ws)

⅜" (1 cm)

Sew each half separately without stitching through seam allowance

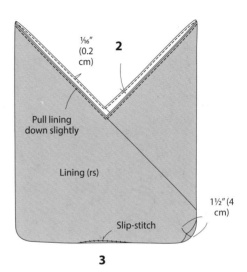

¹⁄₁₆" (0.2 cm)

2

Pull lining down slightly

Lining (rs)

1½" (4 cm)

Slip-stitch

3

Finish the bag

Fold in each side on one of the triangular points at the top of the bag. Thread both bamboo rings on, then fold the fabric to the inside of the bag. Stitch to the lining to secure. To complete the handle, thread the other triangular point through the bamboo rings.

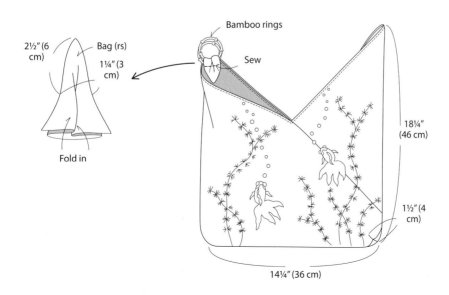

2½" (6 cm)

Bag (rs)

1¼" (3 cm)

Fold in

Bamboo rings

Sew

18¼" (46 cm)

1½" (4 cm)

14¼" (36 cm)

MATERIALS

Fabric
- Bag: 22¾" x 31½" (58 x 80 cm) of red and beige polka dot georgette
- Lining: 22¾" x 31½" (58 x 80 cm) of dark green silk taffeta

Interfacing
- Featherweight fusible: 8¾" x 30¾" (22 x 78 cm)

Embroidery Supplies
- 60 weight sewing machine thread in red
- Four hundred two ⅜" x ⅜" (0.8 x 0.8 cm) square iridescent sequins

CUTTING INSTRUCTIONS

- **Seam allowance is not included. Add ⅜" (1 cm) seam allowance to all piece edges, unless otherwise noted.**
- Trace and cut out the bag, bag interfacing, and lining interfacing templates on pattern sheet B. Cut out each piece according to the diagrams below.

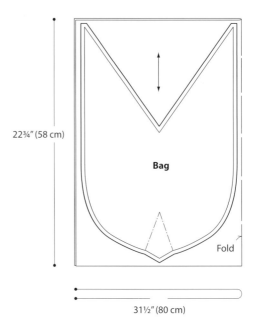

22¾" (58 cm)

Bag

Fold

31½" (80 cm)

Cut 2 bags from each:
Bag fabric and lining fabric

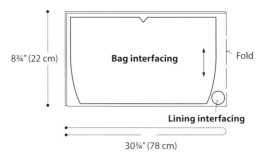

8¾" (22 cm)

Bag interfacing

Fold

Lining interfacing

30¾" (78 cm)

Cut 2 bag interfacings without seam allowance from:
Featherweight fusible interfacing
Cut 2 lining interfacings without seam allowance from:
Featherweight fusible interfacing

CONSTRUCTION STEPS

> **Sew using ⅜" (1 cm) seam allowance, unless otherwise noted.**

Adhere the interfacing

Adhere featherweight fusible interfacing to the wrong side of each bag piece. Only apply interfacing to the area that will be embroidered.

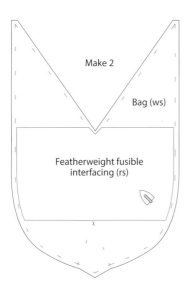

Embroider the bag with sequins

Embroider the bag pieces with sequins, following the placement indicated on pattern sheet B. Refer to page 52 for instructions on attaching the sequins.

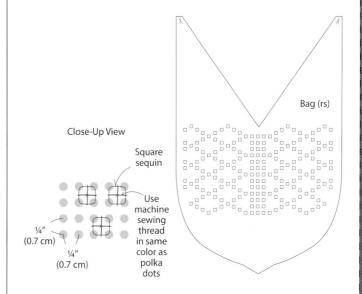

Sew the darts

Sew the darts on both bag pieces and lining pieces.

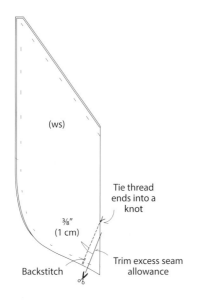

Sew the bag together

Align the two bag pieces with right sides together and sew along sides and bottom.

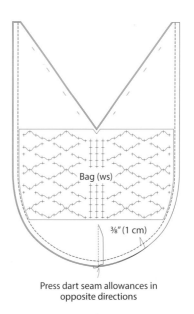

Make the lining

1 Adhere circular piece of featherweight fusible interfacing to the wrong side of each lining piece.

2 Align the two lining pieces with right sides together and sew along sides and bottom, leaving a 4" (10 cm) opening for turning right side out.

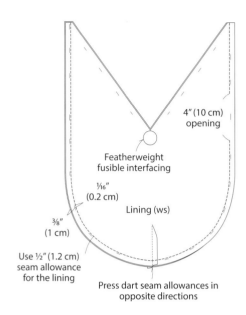

4" (10 cm) opening

Featherweight fusible interfacing

¹⁄₁₆" (0.2 cm)

Lining (ws)

³⁄₈" (1 cm)

Use ½" (1.2 cm) seam allowance for the lining

Press dart seam allowances in opposite directions

Attach the lining

1 Align the bag and lining with right sides together and sew along the bag opening. Make clips into the seam allowance at the points.

2 Turn the bag right side out. Topstitch around the bag opening, pulling the lining down slightly as you stitch so a bit of the bag fabric is visible on the inside.

3 Slip-stitch the opening closed. Tie the triangular points into a knot to complete the handle.

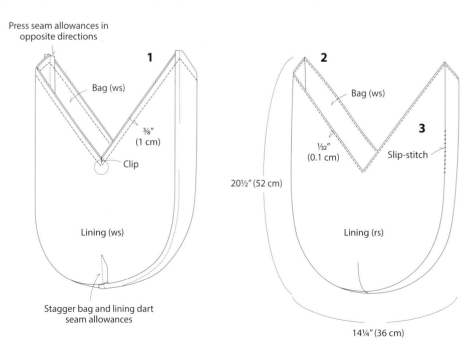

Press seam allowances in opposite directions

1

Bag (ws)

³⁄₈" (1 cm)

Clip

Lining (ws)

Stagger bag and lining dart seam allowances

2

Bag (ws)

¹⁄₃₂" (0.1 cm)

3

Slip-stitch

20½" (52 cm)

Lining (rs)

14¼" (36 cm)

MATERIALS

Bag
- Black straw bag with 32¾" (83 cm) opening circumference

Fabric
- Lining: 6¾" x 39½" (17 x 100 cm) of black and white polka dot cotton
- Appliqué: 4" x 8" (10 x 20 cm) each of thick beige cotton and tan linen

Interfacing
- Lightweight fusible: 6¾" x 39½" (17 x 100 cm)
- Fusible canvas: 2" x 32" (2 x 81.5 cm)
- Fusible foam stabilizer: 5½" x 5½" (14 x 14 cm)
- Double-sided fusible: 6" x 9¾" (15 x 25 cm)

Embroidery Supplies
- Avril cotton gima in white (1)
- ¼" (0.4 cm) diameter cotton string in white
- 60 weight sewing machine thread in black, beige, and tan

Handle
- Two ⅝" x 16½" (1.5 x 42 cm) black fabric handles with beige netting

CUTTING INSTRUCTIONS

- **Seam allowance is not included. Add ⅜" (1 cm) seam allowance to all piece edges, unless otherwise noted.**
- Cut out each piece according to the diagrams below.

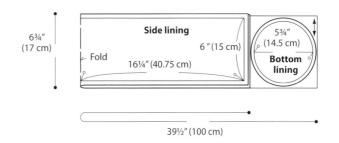

Cut 1 side lining and 1 bottom lining from each:
Lining fabric and lightweight fusible interfacing

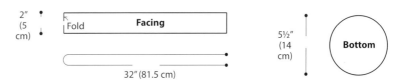

Cut 1 facing without seam allowance from:
Fusible canvas

Cut 1 bottom without seam allowance from:
Fusible foam stabilizer

CONSTRUCTION STEPS

Sew using ⅜" (1 cm) seam allowance, unless otherwise noted.

Appliqué and embroider the bag

Follow the instructions on pages 42–43 and pattern sheet A to appliqué and embroider the bag. Refer to the diagram at right for placement. Use the same color thread as the appliqué fabric to machine appliqué with zigzag stitch.

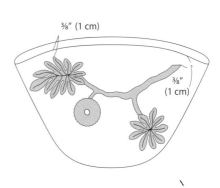

Make the lining

1   Adhere lightweight fusible interfacing to the wrong side of the side and bottom linings. Fold the side lining in half and sew into a tube. Press seam allowance open.

2   With right sides together, align side and bottom linings at marks and pin.

3   Fold ¼" (0.5–0.6 cm) pleats on the side lining until it is the same size as the bottom lining (about 32 pleats).

4   Sew the side and bottom linings together.

5   Adhere fusible canvas interfacing to the wrong side of the side lining along the bag opening.

6   Sew the fusible foam stabilizer to the wrong side of the bottom lining.

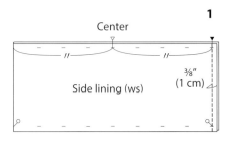

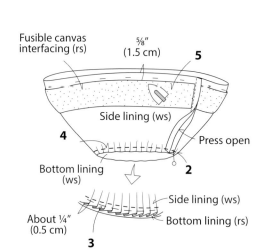

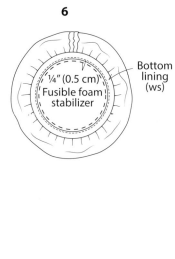

Finish the bag

1   Insert the lining into the straw bag. Fold the seam allowances in and slip-stitch the bag and lining together around the opening, leaving openings at the handle attachment positions noted in the diagram at right. As you stitch, pull the lining down slightly so a bit of the bag is visible on the inside.

2   Insert the handles into the openings and topstitch 2–3 times to secure. Use black for your top thread and white for your bottom thread and sew from the outside of the bag.

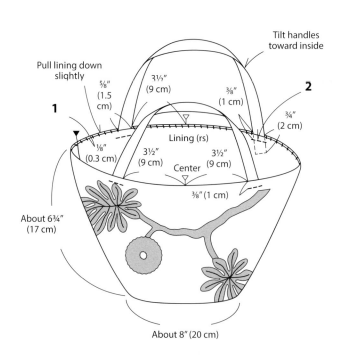

Beaded Brooches SHOWN ON PAGE 22

MATERIALS

Variation 3

- Main fabric: 6" x 6" (15 x 15 cm) of black linen
- 1½" x 1½" (4 x 4 cm) each of gray leather, lightweight fusible interfacing, heavyweight fusible interfacing, and card stock
- 1¾" x 2¼" (4.5 x 5.5 cm) of DMC 14 count soluble canvas
- 11/0 glass seed beads (such as Miyuki Delica) in brown (65), black (310), off-white (353), green (877), and 2 shades of red (362, 654)
- One 1½" (3.5 cm) long brooch pin
- Cotton stuffing
- Quick-dry tacky glue

FINISHED SIZES

- Variation 1: 1½" x 2½" (4 x 6 cm)
- Variation 2: 1½" x 2¼" (3.5 x 5.5 cm)
- Variation 3: 1½" (4 cm) diameter
- Variation 4: 1½" (4 cm) diameter
- Variation 5: 1" x 1½" (2.5 x 3.5 cm)

Materials for additional project variations on page 91

CUTTING INSTRUCTIONS

Trace and cut out the brooch templates on pattern sheet D. Use the templates to cut out the card stock, leather, and heavyweight fusible interfacing. Note: Do not cut out the main fabric or lightweight fusible interfacing. You will interface and embroider each piece before trimming into shape using the template.

CONSTRUCTION STEPS

> These instructions use Variation 3 as an example. Follow the same process for all brooch variations.

Make the foundation

Glue the stuffing to the card stock to create a foundation that is about ¾" (2 cm) thick. Note: The stuffing will compress to ⅜" (1 cm) thick when covered with fabric.

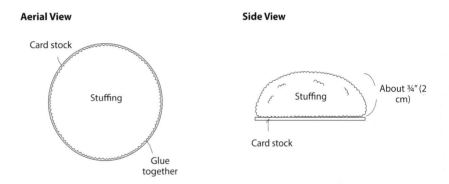

Adhere the interfacing

Align the centers of the lightweight fusible interfacing and the main fabric. Adhere the interfacing to the wrong side of the fabric.

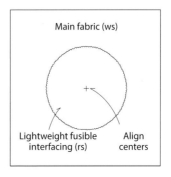

Embroider the brooch

1 Align the centers of the soluble canvas and the main fabric. Baste.

2 Embroider with beads following the chart on page 92. Refer to page 47 for detailed beaded embroidery instructions.

3 Dissolve the canvas in water according to the manufacturer's instructions. Dry the embroidery by ironing from the wrong side of the work.

4 Use the template to trim the main fabric into shape.

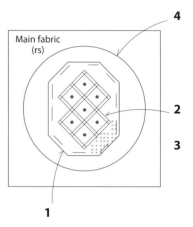

Main fabric (rs)

4

2

3

1

Cover the foundation

1 Running stitch around the main fabric using ⅛" (0.3 cm) seam allowance.

2 Align the main fabric on top of the foundation. Pull thread ends to gather the main fabric around the foundation. Tighten to compress the stuffing to ⅜" (1 cm), or about half its original thickness, then knot.

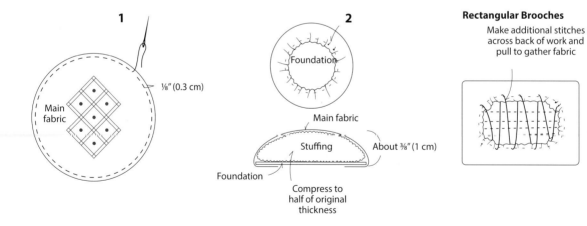

1

Main fabric

⅛" (0.3 cm)

2

Foundation

Main fabric

Stuffing

About ⅜" (1 cm)

Foundation

Compress to half of original thickness

Rectangular Brooches
Make additional stitches across back of work and pull to gather fabric

Make the brooch back

1 Adhere heavyweight fusible interfacing to the wrong side of the leather.

2 Use a pin to score the right side of the leather at the position to attach the brooch pin.

3 Glue the brooch pin to the leather.

4 Secure each side of the brooch pin with two thread tacks.

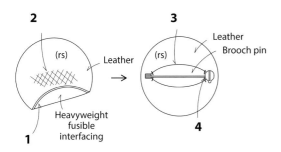

Finish the brooch

Glue the foundation to the wrong side of the brooch back.

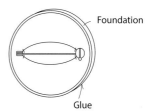

MATERIALS FOR ADDITIONAL PROJECT VARIATIONS

Variation 1
- Main fabric: 6" x 6" (15 x 15 cm) of unbleached cotton gabardine
- 1½" x 2½" (4 x 6 cm) each of gray leather, lightweight fusible interfacing, heavyweight fusible interfacing, and card stock
- 2" x 3" (5 x 7.5 cm) of DMC 14 count soluble canvas
- 11/0 glass seed beads (such as Miyuki Delica) in 2 shades each of green (656, 877), blue (217, 798), and gray (338, 652), 1 shade each of pink (1376) and black (310), and 3 shades of purple (281, 361, 661)
- One 1¾" (4.2 cm) long brooch pin
- Cotton stuffing
- Quick-dry tacky glue

Variation 2
- Main fabric: 6" x 6" (15 x 15 cm) of unbleached cotton gabardine

- 1½" x 2¼" (3.5 x 5.5 cm) each of gray leather, lightweight fusible interfacing, heavyweight fusible interfacing, and card stock
- 2" x 3" (5 x 7.5 cm) of DMC 14 count soluble canvas
- 11/0 glass seed beads (such as Miyuki Delica) in red (378), black (310), and blue (378)
- One 1¼" (3 cm) long brooch pin
- Cotton stuffing
- Quick-dry tacky glue

Variation 4
- Main fabric: 6" x 6" (15 x 15 cm) of green silk taffeta
- 1½" x 1½" (4 x 4 cm) each of gray leather, lightweight fusible interfacing, heavyweight fusible interfacing, and card stock
- 2" x 2¼" (5 x 5.5 cm) of DMC 14 count soluble canvas
- 11/0 glass seed beads (such as

Miyuki Delica) in clear (673), black (310), and 2 shades of pink (281, 1376)
- One 1" (2.5 cm) long brooch pin
- Cotton stuffing
- Quick-dry tacky glue

Variation 5
- Main fabric: 6" x 6" (15 x 15 cm) of gray linen
- 1½" x 2" (4 x 5 cm) each of gray leather, lightweight fusible interfacing, heavyweight fusible interfacing, and card stock
- 1½" x 2" (4 x 5 cm) of DMC 14 count soluble canvas
- 11/0 glass seed beads (such as Miyuki Delica) in white (335) and purple (361)
- One 1" (2.5 cm) long brooch pin
- Cotton stuffing
- Quick-dry tacky glue

CROSS-STITCH CHARTS

Variation 1

▽	= 217
M	= 281
■	= 310
✕	= 361
U	= 652
Z	= 656
E	= 661
B	= 798
G	= 877
╱	= 338
▒	= 1376

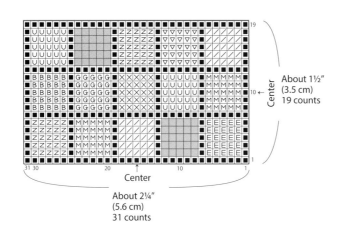

About 1½"
(3.5 cm)
19 counts

Center

About 2¼"
(5.6 cm)
31 counts

Variation 2

■	= 310
▲	= 378
B	= 798

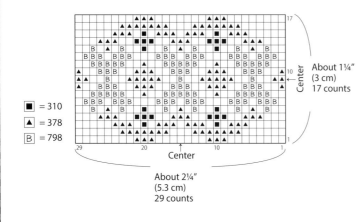

About 1¼"
(3 cm)
17 counts

Center

About 2¼"
(5.3 cm)
29 counts

Variation 3

◎	= 65
■	= 310
△	= 353
Y	= 362
●	= 654
G	= 877

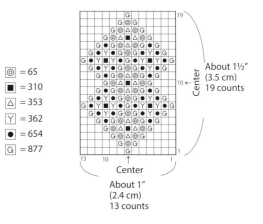

About 1½"
(3.5 cm)
19 counts

Center

About 1"
(2.4 cm)
13 counts

Variation 4

M	= 281
■	= 310
·	= 673
▒	= 1376

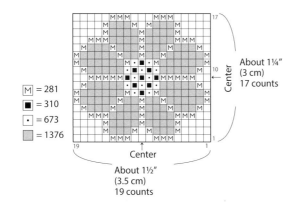

About 1¼"
(3 cm)
17 counts

Center

About 1½"
(3.5 cm)
19 counts

Variation 5

O	= 335
✕	= 361

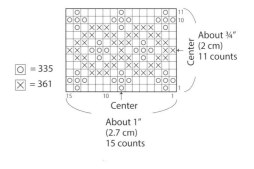

About ¾"
(2 cm)
11 counts

Center

About 1"
(2.7 cm)
15 counts

MATERIALS

Fabric
- Bag: 15½" x 31½" (39 x 80 cm) of blue and beige checkered thick cotton
- Lining: 15½" x 37" (39 x 94 cm) of navy thick cotton

Interfacing
- Medium-weight fusible: 15½" x 31½" (39 x 80 cm)
- Lightweight fusible: 15½" x 37" (39 x 94 cm)
- Double-sided fusible: 8" x 9¾" (20 x 25 cm)
- Fusible canvas: 9" x 27½" (23 x 70 cm)
- Fusible foam stabilizer: 2¾" x 9¾" (7 x 25 cm)

Embroidery Supplies
- DANSK Blomstergarn in A: white (1), B: black (16), C: lilac (200), D: brown (606), E: light brown (610), and F: dark navy (709)
- G: DMC cotton embroidery floss #25 in black (310)
- H: DMC Retors Mat in black (2310)
- I: Linen cord in beige

Appliqué Supplies
- Scraps of linen fabric in beige, ivory, light blue, navy, green, dark green, taupe, brown, and purple
- Scraps of white organdy
- 59" (150 cm) of ⅜" (1 cm) wide piping
- Sewing machine thread in coordinating colors to appliqué

Handle Findings
- Two ⅝" x 18¼" (1.5 x 46 cm) white plastic handles
- Four sets of ⅜" (0.9 cm) diameter silver studs

Tools
- Eyeleteer

CUTTING INSTRUCTIONS

- **Seam allowance is not included. Add ⅜" (1 cm) seam allowance to all piece edges, unless otherwise noted.**
- Trace and cut out the front/back and bottom templates on pattern sheet C.
- Cut out each piece according to the diagrams below and on the next page.
- Note: For the front, cut out an 11" x 15¾" (28 x 40 cm) rectangle each of bag fabric and medium-weight fusible interfacing. You will interface, appliqué, and embroider the front before trimming into shape using the template.
- Cut out the following piece, which does not have a template, according to the measurements below:
  – Pocket: 4¼" x 6¾" (11 x 17 cm) of lining fabric and lightweight fusible interfacing

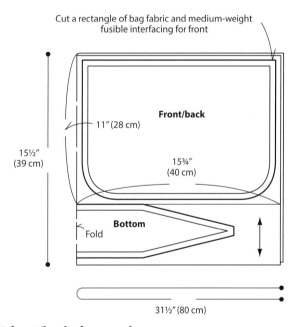

Cut a rectangle of bag fabric and medium-weight fusible interfacing for front

Front/back

11" (28 cm)

15½" (39 cm)

15¾" (40 cm)

Bottom

Fold

31½" (80 cm)

Cut 2 front/backs from each:
Bag fabric (cut 1 as rectangle) and medium-weight fusible interfacing (cut 1 as rectangle)

Cut 2 bottoms from each:
Bag fabric and medium-weight fusible interfacing

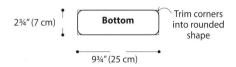

2¾" (7 cm)

Bottom

Trim corners into rounded shape

9¾" (25 cm)

Cut 1 bottom without seam allowance from:
Fusible foam stabilizer

CUTTING INSTRUCTIONS (CONTINUED)

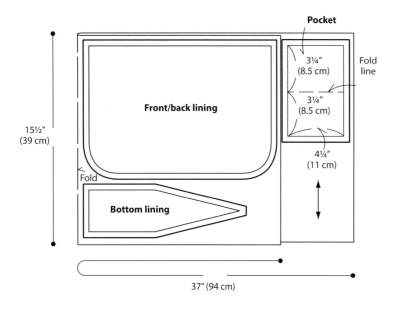

Cut 2 front/back linings from each:
Lining fabric and lightweight fusible interfacing

Cut 2 bottom linings from each:
Lining fabric and lightweight fusible interfacing

Cut 1 pocket from each:
Lining fabric and lightweight fusible interfacing

CONSTRUCTION STEPS

Sew using ⅜" (1 cm) seam allowance, unless otherwise noted.

Adhere the interfacing

1 Adhere a rectangular medium-weight interfacing piece to the wrong side of the rectangular front piece.

2 Adhere medium-weight fusible interfacing to the wrong side of the back and lightweight fusible interfacing to the wrong side of both the front/back linings.

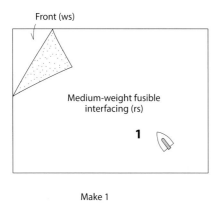

Make 1

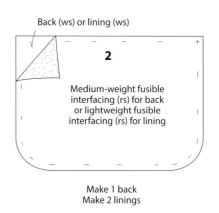

Make 1 back
Make 2 linings

Adhere the interfacing (continued)

3 Adhere medium-weight fusible interfacing to the wrong side of the bottom and lightweight fusible interfacing to the wrong side of the bottom linings.

4 Adhere lightweight fusible interfacing to the wrong side of the pocket.

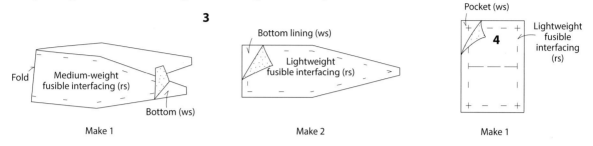

Make 1 | Make 2 | Make 1

Appliqué and embroider

1 Adhere double-sided fusible interfacing to the wrong side of each appliqué fabric. Follow instructions on pages 42–43 to appliqué, following placement indicated on pattern sheet C. Use sewing machine thread in coordinating colors to attach appliqué fabric. Embroider as shown on the pattern sheet.

2 Once embroidery and appliqué are complete, use the template to trim the front into shape, leaving ⅜" (1 cm) seam allowance.

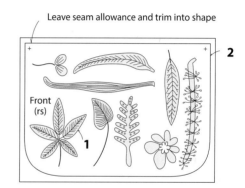

Attach the piping

Baste the piping to the right side of both the front and bottom, as shown in the diagrams below.

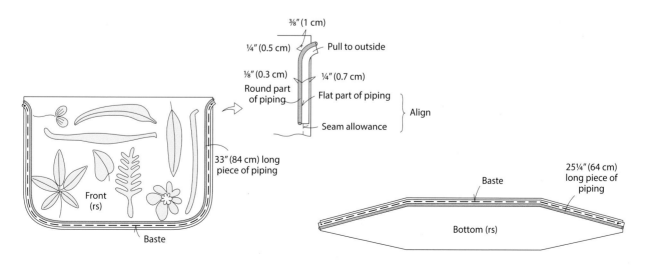

Sew the bag together

1 Align the front and bottom with right sides together and sew from mark to mark.

2 Align the back and other side of the bottom with right sides together and sew from mark to mark.

3 Sew the front and back together above the marks, making sure not to catch the seam allowance from step 2. Press the seam allowances open.

1

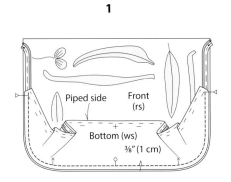

Adhere the fusible canvas interfacing

Use the front/back template to cut a piece of fusible canvas interfacing without seam allowance. Turn the bag right side out. Adhere the fusible canvas interfacing to the wrong side of the bag back.

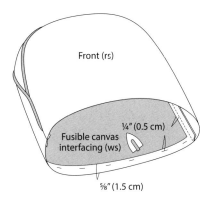

Make the pocket

1 Fold the pocket in half with right sides together and sew, leaving a 2" (5 cm) opening. Turn right side out and fold the seam allowance in. Press.

2 Position the pocket on one of the lining pieces following the placement shown in the diagram below. Topstitch.

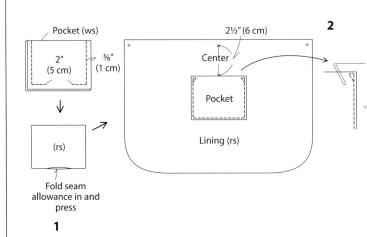

Make the lining

1   Align the two bottom linings with right sides together and sew along the straight edge. Press the seam allowance open.

2   Make the lining following the same process used to sew the bag together, but use ½" (1.2 cm) seam allowance.

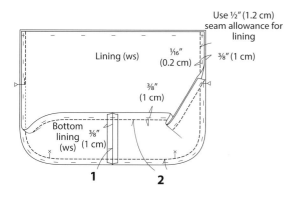

Use ½" (1.2 cm) seam allowance for lining

Lining (ws)

¹⁄₁₆" (0.2 cm)   ⅜" (1 cm)

⅜" (1 cm)

Bottom lining (ws)   ⅜" (1 cm)

1   **2**

Attach the fusible foam stabilizer

1   Fold the bag opening seam allowance over ⅜" (1 cm) on both the lining and bag and press.

2   Adhere the fusible foam stabilizer to the wrong side of the lining at the bottom, then stitch in the ditch on the right side of the lining to secure.

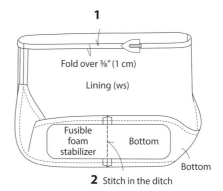

1

Fold over ⅜" (1 cm)

Lining (ws)

Fusible foam stabilizer   Bottom

Bottom

2 Stitch in the ditch

Finish the bag

1   Insert the lining into the bag. Fold the seam allowances in and slip-stitch the bag and lining together around the opening, leaving openings at the handle attachment positions. As you stitch, pull the lining down slightly so a bit of the bag fabric is visible on the inside.

2   Use an eyeleteer to make holes for the handles following placement indicated on pattern sheet C.

3   Make holes in each handle following placement indicated in diagram below.

4   Align the holes in the handles with the holes in the bag and insert studs to secure in place.

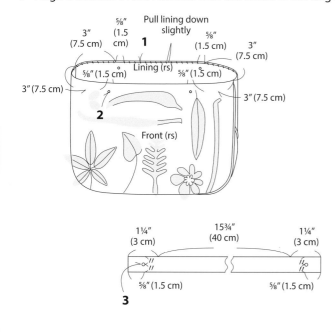

⅝" (1.5 cm)   Pull lining down slightly

3" (7.5 cm)   ⅝" (1.5 cm)   3" (7.5 cm)

⅝" (1.5 cm)   Lining (rs)   ⅝" (1.5 cm)

3" (7.5 cm)   **1**

3" (7.5 cm)

2

Front (rs)

1¼" (3 cm)   15¾" (40 cm)   1¼" (3 cm)

⅝" (1.5 cm)   ⅝" (1.5 cm)

3

4

Bag (rs)

Handle

Align holes and insert studs

Tilt handle toward inside

9½" (24 cm)

3⅛" (8 cm)

14¼" (36 cm)

Raffia Rainbow Tote SHOWN ON PAGE 26

MATERIALS

Fabric
- Bag: 13" x 32¼" (33 x 82 cm) of beige linen
- Lining: 13" x 36¾" (33 x 93 cm) of blue and beige striped thick cotton

Interfacing
- Medium-heavyweight fusible: 13" x 32¼" (33 x 82 cm)
- Fusible foam stabilizer: 2½" x 11¼" (6 x 28.5 cm)

Embroidery Supplies
- Genuine raffia in A: medium blue, B: light purple, C: dark brown, D: green, E: light orange, F: gray, G: mint, H: beige, I: yellow, J: navy blue, K: light green, L: bright orange, M: aqua, and N: black

Handle
- One 17¾" (45 cm) long red leather handle set

CUTTING INSTRUCTIONS

- **Seam allowance is not included. Add ⅜" (1 cm) seam allowance to all piece edges, unless otherwise noted.**
- Templates are not included for this project. Cut out each piece according to the diagrams below.
- Note: For the front/back, cut out two 13" x 16¼" (33 x 41 cm) rectangles each of bag fabric and medium-heavyweight fusible interfacing. You will interface and embroider each piece before trimming into shape using the template.

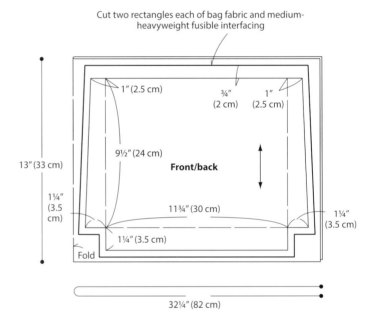

Cut two rectangles each of bag fabric and medium-heavyweight fusible interfacing

Cut 2 front/backs from each:
Bag fabric (cut as rectangles) and medium-heavyweight fusible interfacing (cut as rectangles)

Cut 1 bottom foundation without seam allowance from:
Fusible foam stabilizer

Cut 2 linings from:
Lining fabric

Cut 1 pocket from:
Lining fabric

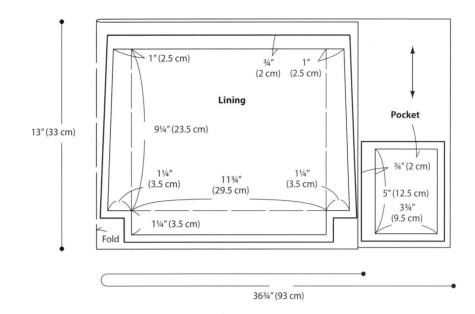

13" (33 cm)

1" (2.5 cm)

¾" (2 cm)   1" (2.5 cm)

Lining

9¼" (23.5 cm)

1¼" (3.5 cm)   11¾" (29.5 cm)   1¼" (3.5 cm)

1¼" (3.5 cm)

Fold

36¾" (93 cm)

Pocket

¾" (2 cm)

5" (12.5 cm)
3¾" (9.5 cm)

CONSTRUCTION STEPS

Sew using ⅜" (1 cm) seam allowance, unless otherwise noted.

Adhere the interfacing and embroider

1   Adhere a rectangular medium-heavyweight fusible interfacing piece to the wrong side of both rectangular front/back pieces.

2   Transfer the embroidery motifs on pattern sheet D to the front and back. Follow the instructions on pages 44–45 and pattern sheet D to embroider the bag. Make a template of the front/back following the dimensions listed in the diagram on page 98. Use the template to trim the front/back into shape, leaving seam allowances as noted.

Front   **Back**

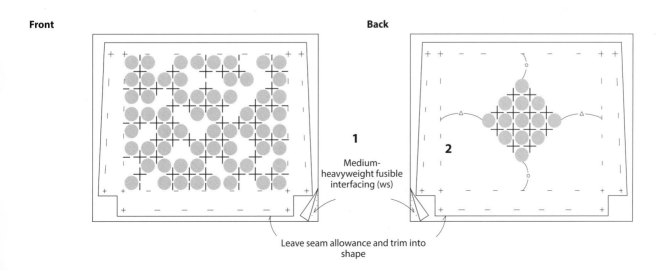

1

Medium-heavyweight fusible interfacing (ws)

2

Leave seam allowance and trim into shape

Make the pocket

1 Fold the pocket opening edge over twice and sew.

2 Fold the seam allowance in on the remaining three edges and press.

3 Position the pocket on one of the lining pieces following placement shown in the diagram below. Topstitch using 1/32" (0.1 cm) seam allowance.

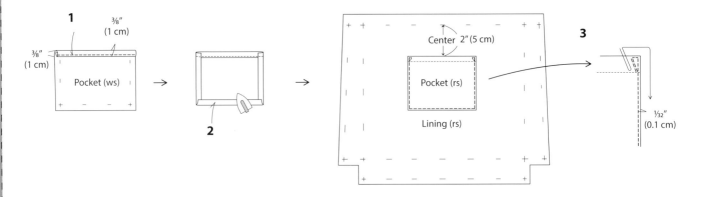

Sew the bag together

Align the front and back with right sides together and sew along the sides and bottom. Follow the same process to sew the lining together. Press the seam allowances open.

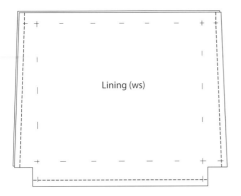

Lining (ws)

Attach the fusible foam stabilizer

Adhere the fusible foam stabilizer to the wrong side of the lining at the bottom, then stitch in the ditch on the right side of the lining to secure.

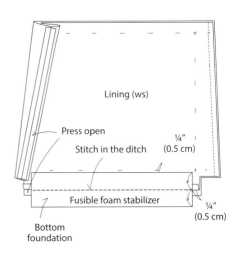

Lining (ws)

Press open

Stitch in the ditch   1/4" (0.5 cm)

Fusible foam stabilizer   1/4" (0.5 cm)

Bottom foundation

Miter the corners

For each gusset, align the bottom and side seam, then sew across perpendicularly to miter the corner.

(ws)

Align bottom and side seam

Press the bag into shape

1 Press both the bag and lining into shape along the side and bottom fold lines.

2 Fold the bag opening seam allowances over on both the bag and lining.

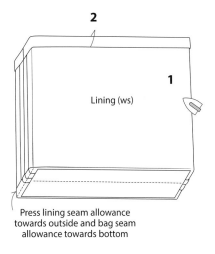

2

1

Lining (ws)

Press lining seam allowance towards outside and bag seam allowance towards bottom

Finish the bag

1 Insert the lining into the bag so that the pocket is positioned against the bag back. Fold the seam allowances in and slip-stitch the bag and lining together around the opening, leaving openings at the handle attachment positions noted in the diagram at right. As you stitch, pull the lining down slightly so a bit of the bag fabric is visible on the inside.

2 Insert the handles into the openings and topstitch 2–3 times to secure.

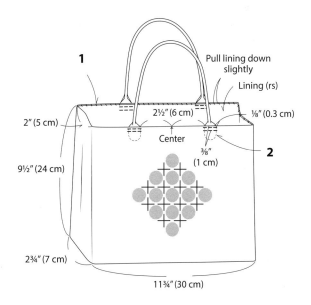

1

Pull lining down slightly

Lining (rs)

2½" (6 cm)

⅛" (0.3 cm)

2" (5 cm)

Center

⅜" (1 cm)

2

9½" (24 cm)

2¾" (7 cm)

11¾" (30 cm)

Ribbon Flower Evening Bag SHOWN ON PAGE 27

MATERIALS

Fabric
- Bag: 8" x 17¼" (20 x 44 cm) of brown silk faille
- Lining: 8" x 17¼" (20 x 44 cm) of light blue silk taffeta

Interfacing
- Medium-heavyweight fusible: 8" x 17¼" (20 x 44 cm)
- Lightweight fusible: 8" x 17¼" (20 x 44 cm)

Ribbon
- ¼" (0.4 cm) wide ribbon in A: light brown, B: light blue, C: purple, D: gray, and E: black

Findings
- Two ¼" x 13¾" (0.5 x 35 cm) dark brown leather cords
- 23¾" (60 cm) of ¼" (0.5 cm) diameter dark brown waxed cord
- Eight sets of ¼" (0.7 cm) diameter grommets
- One ⅜" (0.9 cm) diameter disc-shaped bead
- Two ⅜" x ⅝" (0.8 x 1.5 cm) gourd-shaped beads

Tools
- Eyeleteer

CUTTING INSTRUCTIONS

- **Seam allowance is not included. Add ⅜" (1 cm) seam allowance to all piece edges, unless otherwise noted.**
- Trace and cut out the bag template on pattern sheet B. Cut out each piece according to the diagram below.
- Note: For the bag, cut out two 8" x 8¾" (20 x 22 cm) rectangles each of bag fabric and medium-heavyweight fusible interfacing. You will interface and embroider each piece before trimming into shape using the template.

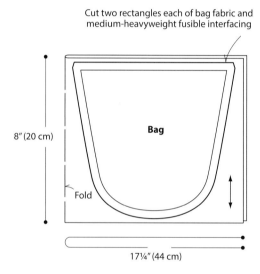

Cut two rectangles each of bag fabric and medium-heavyweight fusible interfacing

8" (20 cm)

Bag

Fold

17¼" (44 cm)

Cut 2 bags from each:
Bag fabric (cut as rectangles) and medium-heavyweight fusible interfacing (cut as rectangles), lining fabric, and lightweight fusible interfacing

CONSTRUCTION STEPS

Sew using ⅜" (1 cm) seam allowance, unless otherwise noted.

Adhere the interfacing

1   Adhere a rectangular medium-heavyweight fusible interfacing piece to the wrong side of both rectangular bag pieces.

2   Adhere lightweight fusible interfacing to the wrong side of both lining pieces.

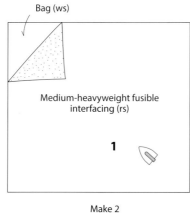

Bag (ws)

Medium-heavyweight fusible interfacing (rs)

1

Make 2

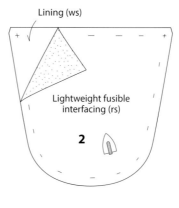

Lining (ws)

Lightweight fusible interfacing (rs)

2

Make 2

Embroider the bag

1   Transfer the embroidery motif on pattern sheet B onto each bag piece. Embroider as indicated on the pattern sheet. Refer to page 53 for instructions on ribbon embroidery.

2   Once the embroidery is complete, use the template to trim each bag piece into shape, leaving ⅜" (1 cm) seam allowance.

2 Leave seam allowance and trim into shape

1

Make 2

Sew the bag together

1 Align the two bag pieces with right sides together and sew along sides and bottom. Follow the same process to sew the two lining pieces together, but leave a 2¾" (7 cm) opening to turn right side out.

2 Align the bag and lining with right sides together and sew around the bag opening.

3 Turn the bag right side out and slip-stitch the opening closed. Pull the lining down slightly so a bit of the bag fabric is visible on the inside.

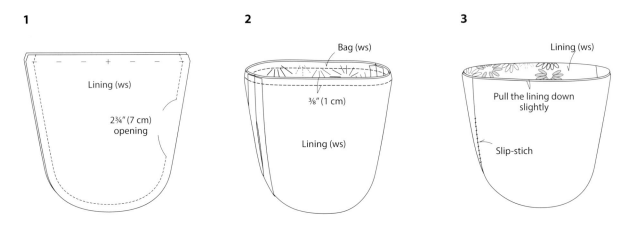

Finish the bag

1 Install the grommets, following placement indicated on pattern sheet B.

2 Use the eyeleteer to make a hole ⅝" (1.5 cm) from each handle end. Thread the waxed cord through the grommets and handles.

3 Thread the waxed cord ends through the disc-shaped bead.

4 Thread each waxed cord end through a gourd-shaped bead and knot.

5 Fold the sides of the bag in and pull the cord to adjust the shape of the bag.

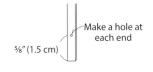

Beaded Wool Purse SHOWN ON PAGE 28

MATERIALS

Fabric
- Bag: 9¾" x 25¼" (25 x 64 cm) of charcoal gray wool
- Lining: 9¾" x 31½" (25 x 80 cm) of yellow, green, and beige plaid silk

Interfacing
- Lightweight fusible: 19¾" x 31½" (50 x 80 cm)
- Heavyweight fusible interfacing: 8¾" x 22" (22 x 56 cm)

Beads
- Small round beads in light blue, dark blue, light green, dark green, pink, cream, and white
- Medium round beads in black
- 6 mm long bugle beads in silver, yellow, and marbled brown
- 4.5 mm long bugle beads in green
- 11/0 glass seed beads (such as Miyuki Delica) in purple, teal, green, turquoise, and metallic purple
- Seven 3 mm round wooden beads in yellow and forty-five in white
- Nine 3 mm round glass beads in light blue
- Five 13 mm circular shell beads with holes in brown
- Eleven 7 mm round rhinestones with two holes
- Two 9 x 11 mm oval shell beads in white
- One 3 x 6 mm oval wooden bead in dark purple
- One 3 x 6 mm oval glass bead in light blue and one in sea foam green

Handle and Clasp Findings
- Two 17¼" (43.5 cm) long pieces of 1½" (4 cm) wide grosgrain ribbon in black
- Six 17¾" (45 cm) long pieces of ⅛" (0.3 cm) wide rope
- One ½" (1.2 cm) diameter wire shank button in magenta
- One ¼" (0.7 cm) diameter support button
- 5¼" (13 cm) of ¼" (0.4 cm) wide flat fabric cord in black

CUTTING INSTRUCTIONS

- **Seam allowance is not included. Add ⅜" (1 cm) seam allowance to all piece edges, unless otherwise noted.**
- Trace and cut out the bag template on pattern sheet B. Cut out each piece according to the diagrams on the next page.
- Note: For the bag, cut out a 9¾" x 12¾" (25 x 32 cm) rectangle each of bag fabric and lightweight fusible interfacing. You will interface and embroider the front before trimming into shape using the template.
- Cut out the following piece, which does not have a template, according to the measurements below:
  - Pocket: 4¾" x 8" (12 x 20 cm) of lining fabric and lightweight fusible interfacing

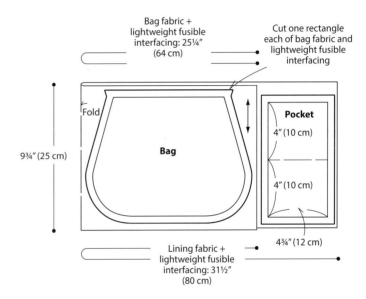

Cut 2 bags from each:
Bag fabric (cut 1 as rectangle) and lining fabric

Cut 3 bags from:
Lightweight fusible interfacing (cut 1 as rectangle)

Cut 1 pocket from each:
Lightweight fusible interfacing and lining

CUTTING INSTRUCTIONS (CONTINUED)

Cut 2 bags without seam allowance from:
Fusible foam stabilizer

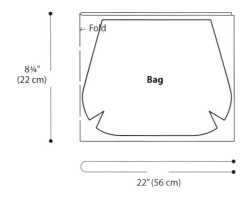

8¾" (22 cm)

Fold

Bag

22" (56 cm)

CONSTRUCTION STEPS

Sew using ⅜" (1 cm) seam allowance, unless otherwise noted.

Adhere the interfacing and embroider

1   Adhere the rectangular lightweight fusible interfacing piece to the wrong side of the rectangular bag piece. Transfer the embroidery motif on pattern sheet B to the fabric. Embroider as indicated on the pattern sheet. Refer to page 53 for instructions on attaching beads. Once the embroidery is complete, use the template to trim the front into shape, leaving ⅜" (1 cm) seam allowance.

2   Adhere lightweight fusible interfacing to the wrong side of both lining pieces and the pocket.

3   Adhere heavyweight fusible interfacing to the wrong side of both the bag front and back.

1   Leave seam allowance and trim into shape

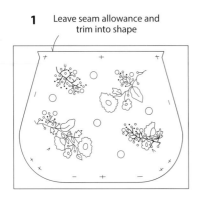

2

Lining (ws)

Lightweight fusible interfacing (rs)

Make 2

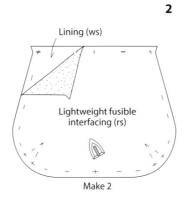

Pocket (ws)

Lightweight fusible interfacing (rs)

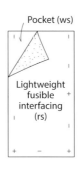

3

Back (ws)

¼" (0.5 cm)

Heavyweight fusible interfacing

Make 2

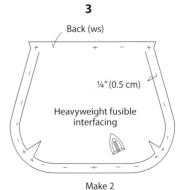

Make the pocket

1 Fold the pocket in half with right sides together and sew, leaving a 2" (5 cm) opening. Turn right side out and fold the seam allowance in. Press.

2 Position the pocket on one of the lining pieces following the placement shown in the diagram below. Topstitch.

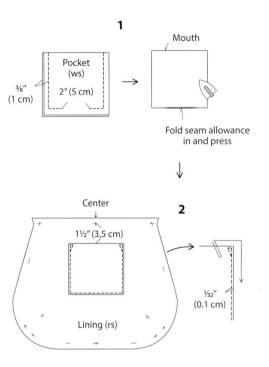

Sew the darts

Sew the darts on both the bag pieces and lining pieces.

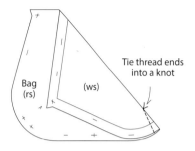

Sew the bag together

1 Align the bag front and back with right sides together and sew along sides and bottom. Before you sew, make sure the darts are pressed in opposite directions on the front and back. Press the seam allowance open. Follow the same process to sew the lining together, but use ½" (1.2 cm) seam allowance.

2 Fold the bag opening seam allowance over ⅜" (1 cm) on both the bag and lining and press.

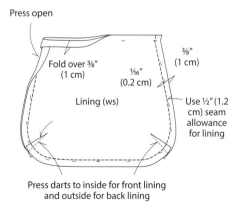

Make the button loop

1 Fold a 4" (10 cm) long piece of flat fabric cord in half.

2 Wrap the remaining 1¼" (3 cm) long piece of flat fabric cord around the folded cord to make a ¾" (2 cm) loop and sew to secure.

¾"
(2 cm)

2

1

Make the handles

Fold each piece of ribbon in half widthwise. Sew to create a tube, then turn right side out. Insert three ropes into each grosgrain ribbon tube and sew in place 1¼" (3 cm) from each end of the ribbon. Trim the excess rope.

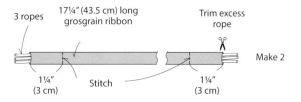

3 ropes

17¼" (43.5 cm) long grosgrain ribbon

Trim excess rope

Make 2

1¼"
(3 cm)

Stitch

1¼"
(3 cm)

Finish the bag

1 Sew the button loop and the handles to the bag opening seam allowance on the right side of the bag, following placement indicated in the diagram below.

2 Insert the lining into the bag. Fold the seam allowances in and slip-stitch the bag and lining together around the opening. As you stitch, pull the lining down slightly so a bit of the bag fabric is visible on the inside.

3 Topstitch 2–3 times on the right side of the bag to secure each handle.

4 Sew the wire shank button to the right side of the front and the support button the front lining, following placement indicated on pattern sheet B.

1

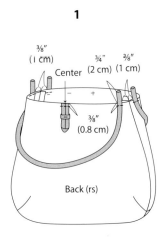

⅜"
(1 cm)

¾"
(2 cm)

⅜"
(1 cm)

Center

⅜"
(0.8 cm)

Back (rs)

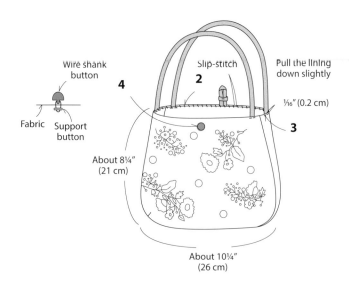

Wire shank button

4

Slip-stitch

2

Pull the lining down slightly

1/16" (0.2 cm)

Fabric   Support button

3

About 8¼"
(21 cm)

About 10¼"
(26 cm)

Striped Clutch SHOWN ON PAGE 30

MATERIALS

Fabric

- Bag fabric #1: 3¼" x 10¾" (8.5 x 27 cm) of purple linen
- Bag fabric #2: 2½" x 10¾" (6 x 27 cm) of light blue linen
- Bag fabric #3: 1¾" x 10¾" (4.5 x 27 cm) of beige linen
- Bag fabric #4: 5¼" x 10¾" (13.5 x 27 cm) of black linen
- Lining: 9" x 27¼" (23 x 69 cm) of light purple tsumugi pongee or linen/silk blend

Interfacing

- Medium-heavyweight fusible: 9" x 10¾" (23 x 27 cm)
- Lightweight fusible: 9" x 27¼" (23 x 69 cm)

Embroidery Supplies

- Kite string in off-white
- DMC Cebelia #20 in off-white (739)
- Cotton gima in charcoal gray
- Ninety-six ¼" (0.5 cm) diameter iridescent white sequins

CUTTING INSTRUCTIONS

- **Seam allowance is not included. Add ⅝" (1.5 cm) seam allowance to all piece edges, unless otherwise noted.**
- Templates are not included for this project. Cut out each piece according to the diagrams below.

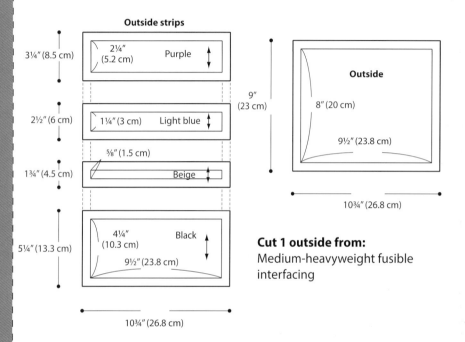

Cut 1 outside from:
Medium-heavyweight fusible interfacing

Cut 1 outside strip from:
Each bag fabric

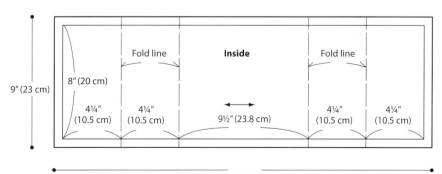

Cut 1 inside from each:
Lining fabric and lightweight fusible interfacing

CONSTRUCTION STEPS

Sew the pieces together

Sew the four outside strips together and press the seam allowances open.

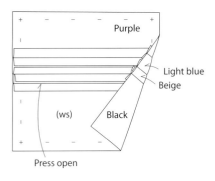

Purple

Light blue
Beige

(ws)

Black

Press open

Adhere the interfacing and embroider

1 Adhere medium-heavyweight interfacing to the wrong side of the outside. Mark the center on the wrong side.

2 Transfer the embroidery motif on pattern sheet C to the fabric. Embroider as indicated on the pattern sheet. Refer to page 52 for instructions on attaching sequins.

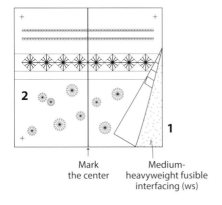

2

1

Mark the center

Medium-heavyweight fusible interfacing (ws)

Make and attach the lining

1 Adhere lightweight fusible interfacing to the wrong side of the lining. Fold the lining following measurements indicated in the diagram below.

2 Align the bag and lining with right sides together and sew, leaving a 3⅛" (8 cm) opening.

3 Turn the bag right side out and slip-stitch the opening closed.

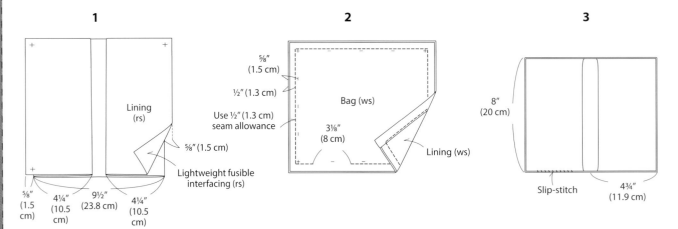

1

Lining (rs)

Lightweight fusible interfacing (rs)

⅝" (1.5 cm)

⅝" (1.5 cm) 4¼" (10.5 cm) 9½" (23.8 cm) 4¼" (10.5 cm)

2

⅝" (1.5 cm)

½" (1.3 cm)

Use ½" (1.3 cm) seam allowance

⅝" (1.5 cm)

Bag (ws)

3⅛" (8 cm)

Lining (ws)

3

8" (20 cm)

Slip-stitch

4¾" (11.9 cm)

Floral Wallet SHOWN ON PAGE 30

MATERIALS

Fabric
- Bag: 8" x 8" (20 x 20 cm) of black linen
- Lining: 8" x 20½" (20 x 52 cm) of green tsumugi pongee or linen/silk blend

Interfacing
- Medium-heavyweight fusible: 8" x 8" (20 x 20 cm)
- Lightweight fusible: 8" x 20½" (20 x 52 cm)

Embroidery Supplies
- DMC Cebelia #30 in white (BLANC), beige (739) and light brown (842)
- Six 3 mm freshwater pearls in black
- Five 5 mm freshwater pearls in white
- Three 5 x 10 mm faceted marquise beads in black onyx
- Five 3 x 5 mm faceted oval beads in black onyx

CUTTING INSTRUCTIONS

- **Seam allowance is not included. Add ⅜" (1 cm) seam allowance to all piece edges, unless otherwise noted.**
- Templates are not included for this project. Cut out each piece according to the diagrams below.

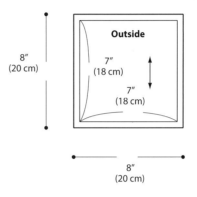

Cut 1 outside from each:
Bag fabric and medium-heavyweight fusible interfacing

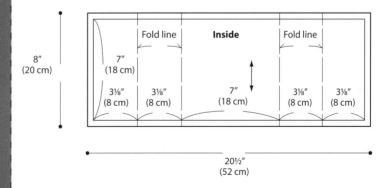

Cut 1 inside from each:
Lining fabric and lightweight fusible interfacing

CONSTRUCTION STEPS

Sew using ⅜" (1 cm) seam allowance, unless otherwise noted.

Adhere the interfacing and embroider

1 Adhere medium-heavyweight interfacing to the wrong side of the outside. Mark the center on the wrong side.

2 Transfer the embroidery motif on pattern sheet C to the fabric. Embroider as indicated on the pattern sheet. Refer to page 53 for instructions on attaching beads.

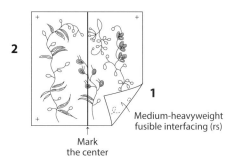

Mark the center

Medium-heavyweight fusible interfacing (rs)

Make the lining

Adhere lightweight fusible interfacing to the wrong side of the lining. Fold the lining following measurements indicated in the diagram at right.

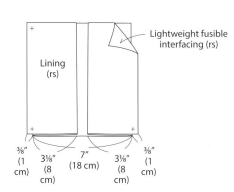

Lining (rs)

Lightweight fusible interfacing (rs)

⅜" (1 cm) 3⅛" (8 cm) 7" (18 cm) 3⅛" (8 cm) ⅜" (1 cm)

Attach the lining

Follow steps 2–3 on page 110 to attach the lining and finish the wallet.

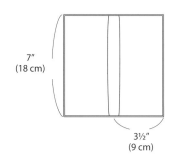

7" (18 cm)

3½" (9 cm)

MATERIALS

Variation 1
- Cotton handkerchief in red
- DMC cotton embroidery floss #25 in black (310)
- 3¾" x 3¾" (9.5 x 9.5 cm) of DMC 14 count soluble canvas

Variation 2
- Cotton handkerchief in beige
- DMC cotton embroidery floss #25 in black (310), blue (930), and brick red (3777)
- 2½" x 3½" (6.5 x 9 cm) of DMC 14 count soluble canvas

Variation 3
- Cotton handkerchief in navy blue
- DMC cotton embroidery floss #25 in ecru (ECRU)
- 2½" x 2½" (6 x 6 cm) of DMC 14 count soluble canvas

Variation 4
- Cotton handkerchief in off-white
- DMC cotton embroidery floss #25 in black (310) and brick red (3777)
- 1½" x 4¼" (4 x 10.5 cm) of DMC 14 count soluble canvas

Variation 5
- Cotton handkerchief in brown
- DMC cotton embroidery floss #25 in black (310), blue (930), and brick red (3777)
- 2¼" x 2¼" (5.5 x 5.5 cm) of DMC 14 count soluble canvas

Stitching Guide

Cross-Stitch

O	= ECRU
●	= 310
△	= 930
☒	= 3777

Holbein Stitch

| ◢ | = 310 |

* Use 2 strands for all stitching.
* Refer to page 46 for instructions on embroidering soluble canvas.

Variation 1

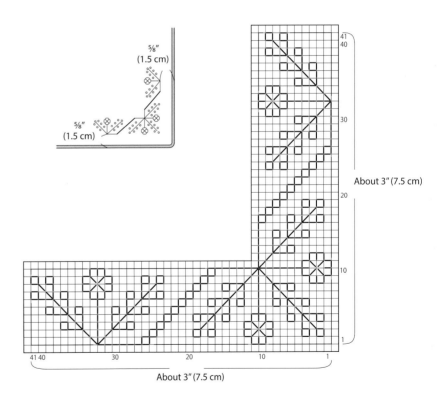

5/8" (1.5 cm)

5/8" (1.5 cm)

About 3" (7.5 cm)

About 3" (7.5 cm)

Variation 2

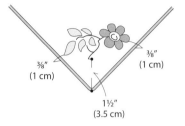

3/8"
(1 cm)

3/8"
(1 cm)

1½"
(3.5 cm)

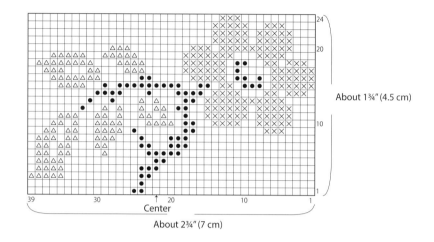

About 1¾" (4.5 cm)

39   30   20   10   1

Center

About 2¾" (7 cm)

Variation 3

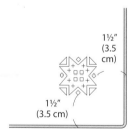

1½"
(3.5
cm)

1½"
(3.5 cm)

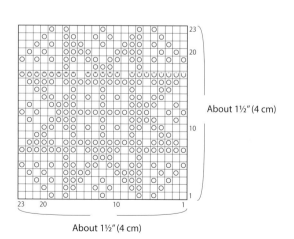

About 1½" (4 cm)

23   20   10   1

About 1½" (4 cm)

Variation 4

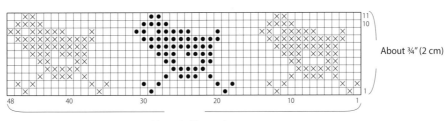

¼″
(0.5 cm)

¼″
(0.5 cm)

About ¾″ (2 cm)

48   40   30   20   10   1

About 3¼″ (8.5 cm)

Variation 5

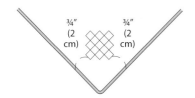

¾″
(2
cm)

¾″
(2
cm)

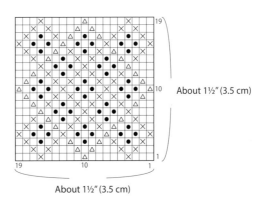

About 1½″ (3.5 cm)

19   10   1

About 1½″ (3.5 cm)

MATERIALS

For Blouse

- Cotton blouse
- Appliqué fabric: Scraps of light blue linen
- Medium-heavyweight fusible interfacing: Scraps
- DMC cotton embroidery floss #25 in black (310)
- DMC Cebelia #30 in beige (739)
- ¼" (0.5 cm) diameter iridescent white sequins (8 for each motif)
- 2" x 4" (5 x 10 cm) of DMC 14 count soluble canvas

For Skirt

- Denim or cotton skirt
- Appliqué fabric: Scraps of beige linen
- Medium-heavyweight fusible interfacing: Scraps
- Lace-weight cotton yarn in black
- DMC Cebelia #30 in beige (739)
- ¼" (0.5 cm) diameter iridescent white sequins (12 for each motif)
- ⅜" (0.9 cm) diameter iridescent white sequins (1 for each motif)

CUTTING INSTRUCTIONS

- **Seam allowance is not included. Add ¼" (0.5 cm) seam allowance to the appliqué pieces, but cut the interfacing pieces out without seam allowance.**
- Trace and cut out the circle template on page 117. For both the blouse and skirt, cut out 1 circle of appliqué fabric and interfacing for each motif (do not add seam allowance for interfacing).

Cut 1 circle for each motif from:
Appliqué fabric

Cut 1 circle without seam allowance for each motif from:
Medium-heavyweight fusible interfacing

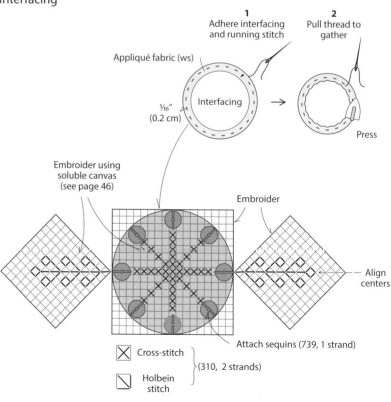

1
Adhere interfacing and running stitch

2
Pull thread to gather

Appliqué fabric (ws)

1/16" (0.2 cm)

Interfacing

Press

Embroider using soluble canvas (see page 46)

Embroider

Align centers

Attach sequins (739, 1 strand)

(310, 2 strands)

☒ Cross-stitch

◺ Holbein stitch

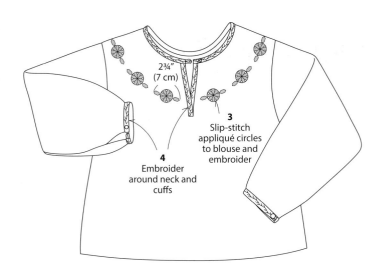

2¾"
(7 cm)

3
Slip-stitch
appliqué circles
to blouse and
embroider

4
Embroider
around neck and
cuffs

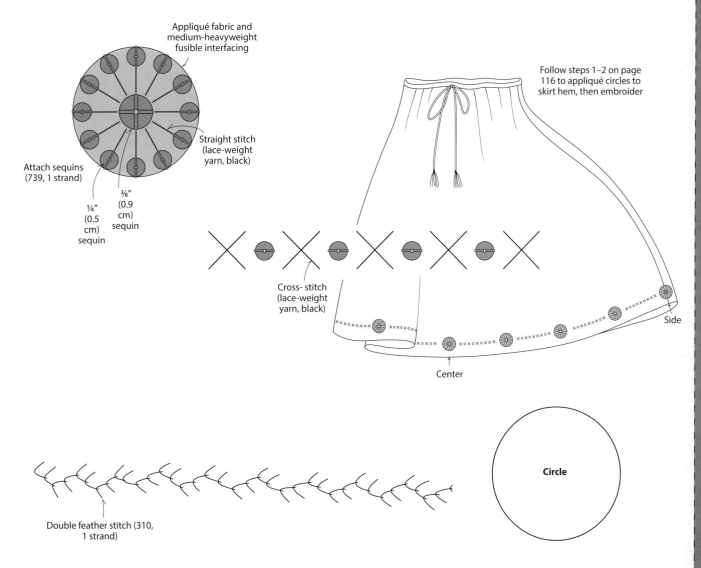

Appliqué fabric and
medium-heavyweight
fusible interfacing

Straight stitch
(lace-weight
yarn, black)

Attach sequins
(739, 1 strand)

⅜"
(0.9
cm)
sequin

¼"
(0.5
cm)
sequin

Cross- stitch
(lace-weight
yarn, black)

Follow steps 1–2 on page
116 to appliqué circles to
skirt hem, then embroider

Side

Center

Circle

Double feather stitch (310,
1 strand)

Resources

B. Black & Sons
http://www.bblackandsons.com
High quality fabrics and extensive selection of
interfacing

DMC
http://www.shopdmc.com
Buy embroidery thread and water soluble
canvas directly from the manufacturer

Fusion Beads
http://www.fusionbeads.com
Large selection of sequins and beads, including
Japanese seed beads

Jo-Ann Fabric & Craft Stores
http://www.joann.com
Arts and crafts store with many embroidery
and sewing products, including DMC thread,
interfacing, beads, and notions

Lacis
http://www.lacis.com
Offers a wide assortment of needles, thread,
and other embroidery supplies

M&J Trimming
http://www.mjtrim.com/
Wide assortment of trims, buttons, ribbons,
frames, closures, and other handbag accessories

Pacific Trimming
http://www.pacifictrimming.com
Great selection of handles, rivets, snaps, chains, and other handbag hardware

Paper Mart
http://www.papermart.com
Sells genuine raffia

Purl Soho
http://www.purlsoho.com/
Great selection of fabric and embroidery supplies, including Appleton crewel wool, DMC, and linen embroidery thread

Nancy's Notions
http://www.nancysnotions.com
Interfacing, marking tools, and other notions

Scandinavian Stitches
http://www.scandinavianstitches.com
Sells DANSK Blomstergarn, or Danish flower thread

VegaKnits
http://www.vegaknits.com
Beautiful yarn, including Avril cotton gima

Add *embroidery & embellishment flair* to your next project

WITH THE HELP OF THESE TECHNIQUE-PACKED RESOURCES FROM INTERWEAVE

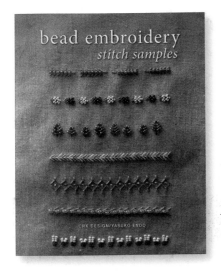

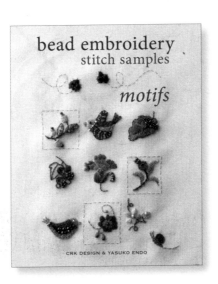

BEAD EMBROIDERY STITCH SAMPLES

CRK Design & Yasuko Endo

ISBN 978-1-59668-760-8, $26.99

BEAD EMBROIDERY STITCH SAMPLES: MOTIFS

CRK Design & Yasuko Endo

ISBN 978-1-62033-610-6, $17.99

HANDSEWN *The Essential Techniques for Tailoring and Embellishment*

Margaret Rowan

ISBN 978-1-59668-756-1, $29.95

shop.sewdaily.com